- Journey through a Soul -

*

Verse
- 1982 -

Book 2

*

TRAUMEAR

*

Paperback ISBN 978-0-244-22593-3

*

www.traumear.com

*

– For those who know how to behave
in the presence of the poetic spirit. –

*

As human beings we develop and evolve. Poets have
the gift to make this intelligible. By means of verse a
poet can give us a running commentary of his own
growth and to the extent that he lives among us his
work, in this genre, can ease our own passage through
the contemporary doldrums. Verse can be a handy
technique for explaining reality in terms of experience.
Those who accept the poet's gift will find the present
work helpful in that direction and to that end.

*

Dreamer and World

You thousand great dreamers of the world,
when will your blood consent to flow
in one vein, not kept apart by
like and unlike, false considerations
of inward drift or outward spell,
behaviour neither cosmic nor too little
enmeshed in the brain's fabrications?
You will honestly entertain doubts

even while the chessboard's configurations
are laid open and made plain.
Your thrifty wills make mountains seem
discordant, plagued by upward thrust,
and the whole earth, that would turn wisely,
must seem to you yet for a time uncouth.
But dreaming is a man's work and should

not be confused with idle scheming,
the treacherous clap-trap hatched for schools
or tossed onto the market to create havoc
and fill purses. It must be done with
open eyes, clear of nocturnal guile,
and none too soon for sport to alter.

Oh catchy phrase, when would you squeeze
your last drop from a morbid carcase?
I have slipped into a foul man's skin
to taste the evil concocted therein
and then, while the flat sea roars
some spiteful orchestration for our ears
beneath there, I may point to the surface.

The cheerful ministrations of the sea
speak much more meaningfully to me
than the crude preoccupations of the deep.
And yet I steer a more adventurous course,
make more discoveries, bring more gold,
for having risked and survived the worst
the sea can offer, tied to its periods.

Let all those who have an axe to grind
mention it to the guardians of the law
whose task is to absorb the ego's jolts.
But leave the sea and sky free for the sailors
and their home-made ships, their dreams of
vital seclusion in some settled harbour
and weakness guided by the strength of hand.

In dreams lies purpose, but the world needs
peace and justice, emotions transformed
for a better hour still, to cushion eternity
and hedge the real field against wear and tear.
Do you not think you too might alter
the way you walk past embracing couples
on the sand, their kisses by surf overwhelmed?

Let their image speak, and their probing hands,
like night plants twisting tendrils round the net.
Do by all means hesitate and observe,
for their lack of an audience is a deep despair,
gnawing once more at their vitality,
and we, accomplished dreamers, may pit
their experience against their falling ways.

Or reach out, where a bough overshadows,
to the love walking beside you in trust,
whose mind and body make yours complete
so silently that beneath your feet
the path vanishes, revealing the stumbling block,
which, recognized, stretches as new path
on solid, sound earth, with a true end.

Come be with me as I force the tide
back from the island's crumbling shore.
All land is island if our view suffices,
the earth itself floats somehow, if you like,
and my dream incorporates all that can be,
all that may happen which love informs
with sovereignty, against non-existence.

Biding my time, watching the terns plunge,
and the sun dissolving too much of cloud,
my memory dashes itself against stone;
this barnacle-encrusted whale, or:
my hope, fleshed out as man and god
stimulates the entire scheme of creation
and proudly all that matters does live.

Father and son stand forth in one example
and show the shape of how one person must live.
Treatment in dream perplexes, and the wild fire
caters to its children, makes them welcome
and teaches them the violent ironies.
The ground swells, the earth heaves
and flames leap from the dark beast's eyes.

Then once more, since carnage was avoided
and sacrifice kept to a bare minimum,
the world makes itself felt and heard,
this time not robbed of its illusion
but rested, meaning that things have weight,
love carries, in my heart resides
reality here personified.

* * *

214

I don't know, I have
some convictions about what one can do with
words by writing them down
or what can be achieved with
written words, but none of it makes
a damned bit of difference afterwards.
I mean you read, or you write,
and you go on to do other things.
I confess I cannot bear
produced passion, performed feeling,
or any other kind of dishonest circus
where elephants are promised but they
turn out cardboard, and the trapeze artist
only talks about his saltos and his swings.
Now mind you, critics need food
but the way they get on you'd think
priests were the be-all and
end-all of churchgoing.
Of course it's up to me
what use I make of the
faculty critical. Nobody
forces me to consult anyone as to
what stands for what either.
Eventually they give me the slip,
these paragons of immortal beauty
and the real estate they leave behind
just has to be occupied by myself.

*

The Statement of
Plautus Maximus, Slave.

I would keep myself detached
for some future program
when the State decides to clear the drains.

*

Plautus Maximus, salvaged from the system
by the honest efforts of his indefatigable spirit,
more accustomed to press his shoulder against
the muddy wheel than to sit back in the cart,
writes this down, pencil stub between grubby fingers,
in the hope that others may profit from what he learned.

*

I grew up a weak child,
fed on what the enemy had left.
My bones were not given a chance.
We trudged from shelter to shelter
while the skies rained fire,
lived with a butcher for six weeks,
on a milliner's doorstep for nine.

Sold into slavery at the age of twelve,
I knew mother and father no more,
learned to stare dry-eyed at
helpful people, sentimental ladies
with baskets hanging from smooth,
white arms, gold in teeth, at
fine-voiced clergymen with black
polished shoes: Learned hate.

*

My wound hurts now and I fear I may die.
But this, an old wound, has refused to heal
these past ten years, and I question my conscience,
fighting premature sleep with the aid of injections,
glad to put up with a degree of discomfort.

I gave in to sleep and they called me traitor.
I ate, to make up for lost time, became a glutton.
When my heart froze I grew angry and unreliable,
to my master's shame, who washed his hands of me.
Through cracks between my eyelids I survey the world.

*

If someone were to bring me water
and loosen these leg irons –
In the moonlight I watched a rat
and I was outraged when I found
I had become one with it.

The ship shudders in its structure,
I have lost track of time's passage,
the same day recurs, foul from
beginning to end.
I have tried to live as an upright man.

The knowledge of moral strength gave me courage
and my Christianity – well – it came and went.
The first man I killed in anger,
the second in self-defence
but the third killing frightened me
because it made no sense.
Another one in me used me to do it
and the recognition of that broke me.

I have never minded being a slave,
I knew where I stood, what I could expect
and what not – until that third killing.
I learned I had a mind and could lose it.

The man's eyes filled with hate for me
and he despised the power I had over him.
Then I became the same as he, hateful;
resentful and hostile throughout.

By killing him I killed myself as I was then,
now I am terrified of such a rebirth
and in that weakness I despise myself.

They have fashioned a huge sail
to conserve petrol as we round the horn.

My pencil broke, it took me an age
to scrape a new point to it
where the rust roughened a pipe
under blisters of oil-paint.

Heavy seas, long swells, rolling
and pitching, drowsing off again.

Barrels broke loose, smashed into the railing.

I try not to pretend pieces of the world,
the Emperor with an ear trumpet to the
mouth of his advisor; a million slaves
and no more public works to keep them
with their hearts to an approved object.

As a human being I am used up.
As an animal I fight the cramped legs,
the itching skin, the pounding skull.
I am a rejected thing,
forgotten under a scrap of canvas,
not any more able to die,
timeless, repetitive like the weather,
no faith in the journey's end.

I hide these notes under my
rag of a shirt, next to my heart.
I want to push things away,
they oppress me, poison the air;
an echo of bitter sorrow.

Bewildered by the contents of my stomach,
my brain builds itself a separate shelter,
my eye turns to lead, looks to the
lowering turmoil of cloud for comfort.
My arms come off at the shoulders,
lie limp on my knees,
terrible to behold,
pieces of myself, as I am now,
the stink of boiling fish in my nostrils,
wafting over suddenly from the funnel vent.

There is an expression:
To have something to show for oneself.
Somebody is bound to find these papers on me,
to judge that their destruction suits me as
further punishment. Could I memorize the lot?

*

I have the entire thing in my memory;
it took some time, and I feel better for it.
Now, if they hang me – nonsense –
they have to hang me, I harboured
the murdering strange one in my body –
as the time draws near I can say to myself
word for word this statement.

I must strive to make it more memorable.

*

I have never aimed very high. My achievements
were limited by my skills in obedience.
The dreams I have when I nod off
make me wish I had stayed alert.

Remember, I can stand up when I like,
shuffle to the end of a yard of chain,
stretch, look over the railing, squat again.
My ankles can separate about sixteen inches.

No one ever encouraged me to learn.
I have heard there are philosophers
who carry the universe in a small basket;
saints, who stand with one leg in heaven,
one on earth; mystics, who can
sleep through life, practicing eternity;
scholars, who die into their books,
sages, who operate to castrate, making
angels out of red-blooded men.

Regarding myself, I view a monstrosity,
rough, hairy, sun-scorched limbs,
legs with scars healed over reluctantly,
bones pulling the yellow skin taut.

If only I could scrutinize my face!
The looking-glass reverses and falsifies.
The fact remains that I stand for nothing.
A perverse joy grips my intestines.

The ship tosses, the slack sheets
slap against the mast, others vibrate.
Dry timbers creak, the morose face
of a stoker, wet with spray, ignores me.

A lot could be said to describe my state
but I prefer to concentrate on private thoughts,
the ordinary resigned self, accustomed to
resignation, desirous of getting through.

By the behaviour of those gulls I can judge
the arrival of a storm, and soon
land will disappear from view again.
They ought to bring me some food.

*

Oh my burning eyes, and the heat
prior to the storm, the close apparatus
of muscle, sinew and bone, or of
hull, rigging and timbers, constraint
to squeeze me tiny like a seed,
seed with the wing of some expressions
and the hope of eventually a release.

The best I can do is make my existence
tolerable, by handing over the extremes
to accident, to confessed ignorance,
to the admission I am someone else,
trapped willingly in his greater reality,
more apt than myself to hold out longer.

The creator embodies himself in each of us
for a time, out of love for the rest of us,
and I have no urge to look or question
beyond that time during which I serve
willingly and content, or unwillingly
and now or later in pain, though pain
comes in any case, only less so if I
kick with the pricks. The ship struggles
more than myself, in a right direction.

Plautus Maximus, one among millions,
fallen on hard times, ruled by his temper
or by stronger circumstance. Worthless slave,
subject to negative quantities, intent on
piecing together at the bottom of the barrel
the three-cornered world. Gripped in a vice
of god's mercy and human justice
with decaying flesh thrown in for keeps.
Surrounded by elements not all noteworthy,
a bit haunted by a deficient past

but able, as a man grown and experienced,
to give in with a vengeance.

The captain's cat grinned up at me
and snuck behind coils of rope,
each strand as thick as my arm.

That was the first flash of lightning.
This is the lull before the storm and
anxious figures batten down the hatches.

Whether I live or die makes no difference.
The pale moon lifts my shadow out of the deck.
Soon these eyes will look on a new morning.

* * *

216

Galatea
(a female angel in distress)

I am not so much astonished by the
complications obstructing my progress,
the serious doubts being put in my way,

as I find myself annoyed
in my inner being
by the unfounded sadness
perpetrated within these celestial zones,

the intimations of an incarnate death.

*

Do look towards the heavens sometimes,
as if you meant to profit from the experience,
not like someone at the local restaurant
booking a table, to devour a lobster
meekly in terms of your civilization,

and see me ride in style, for your sake only.

My steed knows whiteness as his nature's dress,
his troubled eye takes in the various spheres
hastening to their individual postings.

*

But I can tell, you shrink from this.
You demand the contact of hands
and you expect me to grow breasts,
from a sense of duty if at all possible.

But I shall not assist you in this.
My perfection begins where yours ends.
My feet have no quarrel with grass,
yours do. I believe your sort draws up
lists to rally support against enemies.
And what kind of behaviour is that?

It embarrasses you, when you glow honestly.
Some of my relatives grew up in the sticks,
in neglected bush country, emotions'
hinterland, out-back of the freedom fighters,
even there you hazarded a squint.

Angels like me have a right to their
own trimmed sails to take them
swooping protectively over unholy-as-yet
territory, if only because it pleases them.

And it does please me to aggravate you.

*

Look at you! One harsh word
and you suffer from internal bleeding!
Insufficient grit in your diet maybe?

Afraid of a home truth?

Oh, make it easier for yourself,
sell everything you own and
forward the proceeds to Christ.

*

Now you've opened your eyes again, I see.
Isn't language wonderful, even between
such as you and myself, when we trust
instead of rubbing shoulders in a mood!

Our lines of communication should remain open.

*

Let me tell you about the time I spend
wagging my tongue to no account
because of people's sexual aspirations.

Don't get me wrong, I don't consider myself
above or beyond anyone. Look at me,
I can turn myself into a polite person.

*

And all that talk about a better world,
well, it reminds me of the time we were
pressed for space here, not as carefree
as we like, and one disreputable individual,
a dyed-in-the-wool logic chopper with a
hint of dull wits about him, especially
around the eyes, performed tricks to
amuse us; and I swear, we were amused,
legions laughing out loud, sides aching,
and then he came around with his
hat in his hands, demanding, quote,
something a bit more substantial, unquote.

We looked at each other, our spirits sank,
I can tell you. But naturally we decided to
humour him. As soon as you set yourself up
against these mistakes, these basic misformulations,
the agent hardens, stiffens up, practices
cowardly diversion tactics and gives them
virtuous names to boot. Duty, Responsibility,
Freedom, Honour, Patriotism, you know,
notions in black and white that have absolutely
nothing to do with the real thing. Usually
you find them written with capitals and they
stand for labels on hot air balloons – dear
me, I'm getting involved.

*

Listen, I don't mean to interfere with
your way of letting off steam, but
I'd be doing you a disservice if I pretended
too well that I don't care about appearances.

Only glance at these legs of mine,
oughtn't they to be put to some tempting use?
Some of us tend to hide our limbs behind
slightly bad consciences and personally
I don't entirely agree with that. Why be
ashamed of what you can never be held
responsible for? So I've made a bit of a
nuisance of myself by leaning in the opposite
direction and saying: Exhibit your body!
Blushes all around. Beautiful in a way.

17

Incorruptible flesh, some say, has no
business being exposed to faulty eyesight,
but I say: What about those who have
managed, through their own efforts, largely,
to clean up their act? Why should they be
penalized, because that's what you're doing!
Why withhold it from them when they nearly
have a right to it? And let's face it, the
great multitude has had plenty of time and
then some, to make up their mind and adjust.

Well, I know, I can hear you say:
How is that up to you to decide, Galatea –

Alright, fair enough, I'll give you no argument,
but I do have my lights, my sober intuitions,
considering where I stand and in relation to
whom. I do carry messages and not every
envelope is sealed. So if I show off an
ankle or flash a bit of thigh through a
split skirt, it may be I do it advisedly.
The contents of your mind judge you, you
bastards, clinically speaking, no shock for
shock's sake, and when I go on to add that:
      a. not every face has a surface;
      b. the face itself is a surface;
      c. the final appearance is endless;
      d. what you see is not always what
          you look at;
      e, it happens that what you look at
          is what you see;
I feel justified in having said neither too
little nor too much.

*

My body frightens you, and so it should.
I intend to go beyond flesh and blood with you
so that you may participate in terms of flesh and blood,
and of course I do not intend to overlook my
    own interests, speaking tongue in cheek.

I don't like to have to explain so often.
You sit there with your critical faculty intact
as though that were something to be proud of, and then,
when I roll a few indisputable, incorruptible facts into view,
    you blanche, or start an argument with Mother.
Just accept me as someone you can't completely hold.

*

The reason I sound so intelligent is because
I'm talking to you, together we make a
complete scene. Don't get the idea I enjoy
waiting on you, or for you, day in day out.

I'm trapped in your sphere of influence
and unless you give me work
I chase butterflies.

Could be you'll have to settle for
my type of activity in the end.

*

I have reasons for nagging all mortal genius
    until it cries uncle.
Look, I'm going to point towards some ideal place
    and let you whip up your enthusiasm and
    longing for palms, cool streams,
    fireside peace and tranquillity,
    adventure overseas, space conquest:
    you name it, I'll push you – draw you
    towards it, using any hocus-pocus at all,
    and then I'll see that you're forgiven.
    This rubbishy thirst has to be drowned.
    Failure is going to make you love me.
    I'll refuse your presents until you kneel.
    I'm not beyond delusory sweets myself, you know.
    I attack the stars in mid-flight, ruminate over
    the mapped cosmos until it secretes systematically.
    My most favourite transcendentantalizing titbits
    arrive along some rainbow's asexual arch and
    pop into my salivating mouth unpeeled, red lips
    closing softly around them, white arms acting
    as though I had invented the embrace, hair
    in black, oily locks, drunk with swaying, skin
    vaguely transparent, sharp on the intake of breath.

Then I cringe, as though I had
felt some pain – there. It's time
to study the town's lay-out from
that adjacent hill. You may explain
the configurations of streets and
houses to me. I choose, angrily,

where, precisely, I intend to create
benevolent mischief. My thighs
signal my direction to the horse
through his back.

Then I get dressed
by means of an act of the intellect.
Horse becomes horse power times forty
and the asphalt hums under the rubber
on my way to the church picnic.

"Good afternoon, Miss Galatea, pleased you could
come. What a nice handbag! And where is your
young man today? Still interested in that recipe for
oat meal biscuits? Come, we must give you what
pleasure our entertainment allows."

This lady with gentle manners
loves God on Sundays as it happens
and god has noticed. As a result:

due to the ritual of acquired observancies
Christ muses: shall he rededicate his kingdom
to uncracked porcelain with perfect glaze,
or insist, in spite of all the social graces,
and all the culture brewed in timeless casks,
on fingerprints and dropped masks?

Should he, to satisfy a universal craving,
make known to all and sundry how he feels,
allow, for instance, anxieties to creep in,
neuroses to establish themselves, syndromes
to take the floor, complexes to kiss men dead,
or should he tap this lady on the head

saying:

Gentle dame, sweet old dame,
you were made familiar with my name
and the parson wrapped up so neatly for you
Christianity, stuck the flaps down with glue,

copied your gait, wished you well,
flocked with his children to your lavish teas,
now won't you get out of my way, please.

She stares in his direction for a spell,
wonders who spoke, what plucked her sleeve,
freezes, makes mention of me to her cousin
who recently returned from the Foreign Legion.

Someone hands me warm coffee in a cup.

I wonder how long I can keep this up.

Eventually the foundations will have to shake,
cracks will have to appear in the earth's crust.

Am I not sent as good to mortal man,
distinguished from him by my crown,
a force to anoint, no feeble lassy,
for work too brainy, for love too brassy?
A swinger, hankering after a good time?

World, world, you've deserved better.
I'll make my will in earnest one day
to show how spirit subsumes all flesh.

*

Must ask myself such questions as these:
how do most parents today deal with their children.
what do patients in hospitals do with their time.
does copulation at times lead to renewed determination.

Any answer at all to such questions
indicates to me where to insert the wedge,
how to behave to remain out of danger,
what to do to make my life productive.

My wings help me judge topography quickly
and the ability to change into bat, bird or mouse,
causes me problems, since I would remain accountable.
Always my beauty seems to get in the way
of normal procedure: the tooth filled by the dentist,
the attractive setting of the spade mill reproduced,
the subway ride among dead persons through New York.

When my beauty shines forth, thistles are beheaded,
children have accidents, nightmares come true.
Here I have finally, I believe, come face to face
with the nature of my distress, as the topic states.

I refer to the fatal undertow of my accidental
                                        manifestations.

Mortal beauty, aspect of found life,
teases many from the cradle to distraction.

The glory I bear, unpurchased though not unwarranted,
slipped through the roof-tile, oh false absurdity,
threatened to split the tree's trunk, oh superstition,
and now am I called upon to wheel and deal with it?

No, take the image of it away for the moment,
thought of unrottable treasure too, I'd
hold it against the double-viewed world.

Meek and mild maid on milk-white steed, or
miracle-powered insertability of crowned life

in person, as person, meant not to,
never to, bury in itself, under ground,

but from root to fruit in reliance on
what? how? to manage the perfect spear,

to be ever masterful from fatherhood.

Has he not implied as much roundly,
the son, brother, friend, master,
husband of mine and me, through

the three-day blinded, schooled tongue?
Did he not there demonstrate the erosion
of that which lets not glory grow in peace?

For he spake thus out from the whirlwind
of his troubled-to-be-stilled intellect, saying:
I tell you a mystery. We will not all pass away
into sleep, but we will all be changed.

Take that as Galatea's charged example
where substance somehow becomes *the* substance,
now, not after the exfoliation of the metaphor rose,
now, as the imago alights and a petal perhaps
drops, in among the inscrutable bramble thicket.

Imago, flash of sun from sword slicing
the world away from world, as meanwhile
I, Galatea, help shorten the time to time.

And do I have to mention,
am I afforded the opportunity to mention,
my search, at first misguided, for him
who dreams the light of day out into the open?

Daylight become light of day?

Oh youth twice blessed, twice baptized,
twice anointed, twice removed from fire,
patient lamb holding well out to the blade,
be it steel or grass, reaching at once,
bending and stretching before
the vexatious double.

I know fine well who was entrusted to your care
and I'd take full advantage of it.

Yes, I am a mother, the mother of this glory
in my will embodied, the doting mother
of the kingdom's kind here, by my fondness
fetched daily out of the dusty path's heat,
counted up to six on wing, leaf and stone,

held over the font in these words towards world.

*

My love is a man with a clear forehead
and a patient heart.
My love's thoughts centre not on me
but on him who made me.

Where my love sits,
clear eyed under the yew tree,
finches feel safe nearby
and the stoat suns itself on the rock.

As I approach,
in the cool light of the morning,
he experiences no surge of emotion,
neither can I interfere with his state,

for my love lives, in the eyes of all,
not hidden from view, within his conscience.
When he speaks to me, I listen,
and when I speak, his heart's ear opens.

My love is not my soul's image
nor my heart's wishful, empty conceit,
nor a mask I wear when good times forsake me,
nor a popular invention to console my fancy,

nor my mind's ideal, set upon a pedestal,
nor a mood in pictures, to alleviate a crime,
nor yet poor instrument to ease my existence.

My love rises and sets in his season.
He smiles or frowns, his arms lift burdens,
his words please me or they cast me down,
he walks with equal ease through town or meadow.

When my love is glad I suspect no guile,
on his happiness rides no harbinger of disaster.
His hand reaches for me and I do not shrink.

I have grown weary in praise of my love
and the spring from beneath his feet succours me.
It quenches my thirst as his eyes do my desire.

* * *

217

To live one entire day, and then say:
I've lost a day – that's a miser's fortune
and reward. But work one stitch, one chip,
one seed, only let go from the round mind

it, and the stream flows, in can pour,
make that same mind of beauty a thing,
not a self-feasting, fast-sitting beginning,
endless because devoid of rendering.

With the new body think, and therefore let
fruit go, flower close, bud press the white
seed freely, lavish time on it, then reap
long after, several deep sleeps past,

or so you see now, then you'll know how
flesh its self gives, to bar all adultering.

*

Derelict before Breakfast

In this one, I, the poet, of no particular name
but entirely to be used up by what I say,
name included, have an experience to relate.
I thank the one who writes me down.

*

Let me start by mentioning the stony blue
eyes of the man, and how carefully I con-
sidered before risking a look into them

because I feared what might happen.

In retrospect I am displeased with my performance.
Should I have trusted him and spoken my mind?
I did what I often do: stand back a bit and judge.

Even now, I wonder, should I let myself in for this?

A necklace of thoughts, maybe, each bead finished,
that might do, as a picture of the overall effect –
on myself, not you, reader, or listener.

You may do as you please, that's your prerogative.

*

Maybe at the outset I ought to comment
on my primitive disgust when faced with
intentional madness, the screwed up vehemence

that makes us grand in our own eyes.

He banged at the door hard at least eight times,
I was shocked, made mean by the rudeness,
tempted to stay put, dig my heels in, but

curiosity and politeness got the better of me.

A clean looking man, was my first impression,
built broad, thick set, with a massive neck,
his jaunty stance, I thought, not quite genuine,

and those blue-gray eyes, cold and expressionless.

He was looking for someone else. I said: Well,
I don't suppose there's much I can do. Suddenly
he was in the house, complaining, turning

anxiously on his heel, staring at the floor.

It had to do with money someone called Mrs. Thatcher
was taking away from him, and he hated her for it.
That woman, he maintained, is the biggest hypocrite

that ever walked upright on God's earth.

My stomach muscles tightened up. I repeated certain
judgments to myself in my mind. I crept
inside my shell, adjusted the gun-slits and

decided to wait him out.

He'd begun to swagger now, about his days in the North
with the Teddy boys, as a loner, and he could still
hold his head high there. This confused me

because I had taken him for a man of fifty.

The rage he had built up in himself against the Catholics
for not sticking together to hold on to their land
was something else, and me with no great desire

for land or tribe or loyalty.

I noticed that after each outburst of anger, when
he showed how events always justified his passion,
how they told him to leave the shipyards within two days

or be shot, he smiled with satisfaction.

29

and while he smiled his eyes stayed cold like marbles,
but ready to start a fight, with anyone over anything,
only waiting for me, as I judged, to say a word;

I was bound to get my head bitten off over it.

I hadn't had breakfast, maybe I was dull witted,
I could have taken him up on nearly everything he said
but then he searched in his pockets for a slip of paper

with a telephone number, to get in touch with his MP.

Obviously he'd mislaid, or forgotten it, but within seconds
his hands shook, his voice pleaded and he told me
he'd had a coronary, this wasn't good for his heart,

this uncertainty as to that piece of paper.

I'm a stranger in these parts, and hatred repels me,
in myself or anyone else, it frightens me too,
because I can get ready to hate, to hate more, in a trice

and then the worst stands there and grins.

I know, for example, that the new life available today
can't be forced, although we can force ourselves to
make room for it, welcome it, and if a man's mind

controls him, not he it, he is derelict.

That his personality should so much get the better of a man,
a mask of a soul, that all becomes externality
so that fear subdues error and then error rules fear

and parades in front of us, this is monstrous.

*

At the centre of the necklace I turn towards myself.
I am a mass of irritations, faults, dissatisfactions.
I harbour a beast which threatens to destroy me.

My consolation is he who writes this down.

The poet, destroyed by the thing he espoused,
leaves me, the scribe, merely his formalities,
a handful of ceremonies, a ritual, a way of

dealing with the evil he revealed.

I thank the poet for pointing to the reality.
Gratefully I accept his method for dealing with it.
In his absence I regard myself as trustee of his will.

His death made possible our knowledge.

Now scribe and lector are become one vision,
one heart to harvest the fruit of the poet's
courage in conflict, success in self-conquest,

and we follow where his skill created passage.

On the left, the black cliffs of self-doubt overcome,
beneath, the depth of depravity braved,
to the right, the fist of violation objectified,

above, the purest indifference.

and behind, shrieking, accusing illogically,
the shapeless, nameless monstrosity of man's
tragic invention, the ferocity of his failure,

the unmitigated problem of his sight.

The poet knew his sense was blessed
and so he his experience stressed,
for even with his heart's arrest

his vision would maintain.

Our looking under facts and stones,
for which the poet's death atones,
not spill of blood or break of bones,

seems tasteless and profane.

But still, while the illusion lasts
of ideal worlds as plaster casts,
the saint feasts while the martyr fasts

and dead poets rise again.

***

219

Gently seduce the night wind, astutely
make love to the willow fluttering
and swaying in seclusion. Borrow
from the bracing reeds sounds whispered.

*

220

Why do I not more courageously
reach out and do proud
things with my mind brimming?

*

221

Oh be wise, take no more advice from
the limp sages. Their tested domain makes
god's plan look small. Or at least let
the sea's salt spray fling
the season's sunshine with ease
against brown skin. Forget

how once, below stairs, we were tempted,
against bitter tears, by love's
reasoned reproach, and carried downstream

to where the city last was seen
and on its walls the bugler calls
for remedy, the siege by millions.

*

Passion's House

Let passion build itself a house
and there bring sleep around as guest,
no partner in the dreams we fear
nor vision's lack of interest,

but thousandfold escape in joy
from sage's mood and prophet's muse
before the trembling swans their light
as weight interpret and abuse.

Let passion steer its course past reefs
where coral stains blood red the sea;
oh never mind, let passion rest
and come unite your self with me.

I drew a beggar from the shore
one Sunday where the tide had left
his corpse on sand and foul the weeds
embraced his limbs where sore wounds cleft

but nature knew me for my skills
and roused by pity, drawn by love,
showed me myself there, clasped my heart
in god's rich mercy from above.

In memory did I right these wrongs
that now make mockery of my style,
and some men weep to see me stand
so near ancestral graves a while.

Consider how your heathen gods
must technologically survive
or make world sag from sheer lead weight
and leave no earthly thing alive.

In content lies the rest you seek,
in justice the domain you crave.
In my still eye the swans float by,
ignoring beggar, knight and knave.

*

Let passion steer its course past reefs
where coral stains blood red the sea.
Let white sails gleam above the wave
and contest set its teeth in me.

For I am done with wild men's ways
and drowsing by the chimney breast.
Both youth and age have torn my flesh
and simple love has served me best.

The thinking I must do extends
past blessed ignorance, through fire
whose flames expose, in whitened rows
bleached bones, and no time may transpire

before the chief regret of man,
his weak condition, tied to god
by strings of duty, love and fear,
becomes relief; before men prod

their conscience and bestir their will
to limits that are not unknown
and love of enemy, light and truth
has perfect come and easy grown.

The crown of life rests lightly on
the head exposed to crown of thorns
and timid hearts, like cowards, must
surpass the world whose spirit mourns.

The anguish that reflects on souls
impaled by their own jittery fears
makes no one wise, while gods despise
the tyrant's magic, it appears.

We jostle on the earth for space
as though a man were valued here
for air he breathes, for soil he treads
and not for how he deals with fear,

with madness, with insane desire
and how his works come up to scratch,
with critics' spit and Wall street fit
for which no clown can be a match.

*

Dear father, lend my voice such force
as drives these devils from my house,
for passion would live quietly here,
not trick my self and kill my spouse.

Make modest my demands on life
and not too pressing its concerns.
Reject the mockery in my tongue
the eye that squints, the ear that spurns.

Impassive under all sore trials
let me remain, not flinch or squirm.
A steady gaze, a patient back
a constant will to bide my term.

* * *

223

The symbols of reality itself
not of aspects thereof, as time on fire,
stand leaning against each other on my shelf
and out there conquer nation and empire.

Each separate thing, particular and live,
made special by our way of tendering love,
effects, by showing its interior drive,
that we be caused to come down from above

and in each flight of fancy parabolic
confer one more time valid sense and pride
of place and time, in victory apostolic,
on all man's needs – and what he feels inside.

Then what we know as picture and as thinking
becomes real food, for eating and for drinking.

*

224

Blue mist from ground rises
Fairy rings surround mist
Sunshine burns through
Black birds flap wings
Children swing on swings.

*

Crown of polled ash,
round as troll's face,
hole in black sky.

Lovers on park bench,
leaning and clasping,
playful forgetfulness.

*

Spirits on steeple dance,
flood of murk swallow them.
Light from the black tip shoots
upward, where no stars blink.

Turning world – blue roundabout
Playground keeps the children out
Shadow dark beneath the sphere,
Disc of night – no children here.

*

Father the son brings,
turns round and talks,
leaves, runs away,
then no more children play.

* *

225

The spirit wind ruffles
the book's pages.
Clouds drag man's
destiny through ages.

Into distant black holes
worlds disappear.
We would follow,
but we like it here.

*

Vision of open book
haunts the intemperate mind.
Know then that not our eyes
but our souls are blind.

And the wandering Jew
steps livelier with each hour,
by his property tossed
endlessly out of power.

* *

226

The book commands the eyes' attention,
suspicions crowd, I dare not mention.
The lurid picture, bat or mask,
performs suspicion-killing task.

*

227

An eternal realm out here, fastened to light,
and the rainbow bridging from the inn to the earth's end
takes care that time shall not crack, space not bend,
that the heart be consoled, from depth to height,

and the free state of current and force
my terror shall contain, my anguish spray out,
where weeping people and smoking ruins stand about
while wars in obscure hope take their course.

*

12 Verses

I see crumbling all around me
the bastions of authority.
Within, without –
the individual mind
must find authority of another kind.

Where the moon breaks its light
and the sun transmits the sea's reverie
into its own vicinity,
there we loosen the world's spells,
unravelling, not for our sake,
the years' skeins, to please our father.

The shiny sword, small and light
twinkles brightly in the night,
but we our gardens tend
wholly wrapped up in holy word,
not shouting nor staring
at the world's kingdom past caring.

Let those who still bear the rod
insist how the swallow dips and glides
how the bird's shadow flits
along putrid walls
and gradually before wondrous eyes
a sweet rain falls.

Nation and State must be inverted
like hedgehog for fox's appetite.
The radical response,
as here and there the journals show
to the detriment of men who fit
their life to law, has much to recommend it.

Better by far to clasp the stars
in armfuls to the smothered flesh,
to tread the grape, to catch the wind
in cool sails
and if all else fails
discuss it with Jesus.

The embarrassment caused by spoken truth,
the shame that lames the fine intention
because we dread the scandal,
conscience reviled or public remorse,
the pointing finger and the grin
let true love in.

Then action stands, deed is secure
and the grand total of false starts
like lead weight drops
while the final rhymes all fall
into time and place
that no essential piece is wasted.

Come, members of the Corporate Trust,
believers in concerted effort
and magic due to prestige
of honour, name and fame,
take one last look
at the melting face of things to come

and perpetuate in your bones the order
your poor brain would embrace out there
beyond the tendered heart,
the thickened skin,
steeled nerves before the silly devil
who'd rub salt into your wounds.

Put by the pious self-reproach,
gird loins with seasoned self-respect,
abhor the fate
of those who light their lamps too late
or saved no oil
and now their self-spoiled nerves recoil.

I have a mind to bless the earth,
a body to withstand the sky
and heaven to reap,
Christ's word to keep, me free
from harm, tested in eternity's
mantle of real ice and flame.

* * *

229

How arduous to be wakeful in the light
to sustain the tender contact with truth.
So many unidentifiable forces
draw blinds on our existence
and we tend to bed down

on moss covering rock, cushions of thyme
warmed of an afternoon by the sun.
Then sea breezes stream
through our senses, island
dreams derange our fantasy

and we miss the white ship there, hoisting
meaningful flags to evoke our sympathy.
If we were to attract love
as the candle a wayward moth
would reality not seem trite?

* *

230

I am not alone in my
tigerish attempts at cultivating the forest.
If we have relied heavily in the past on
masks damaging the bridges, tragicomic
bombs blowing up the access roads to
the millennium's interregnum, we now

flock in droves, spears held high, across
blood-stained plains, in our hearts
the screaming of eagles, in our sore wombs
unwashed monuments to forgetfulness.

The ethics of culture are hung on the nail,
the landlord pops his head in through the window,
the caged bear has damaged his white claws:

    these three make me what I am.

If the lamplight leaves the stranger unsolicited
so that his crude imaginings romp in the ditch
along with profuse outpourings of demented speech,

how can I help neglecting my mission, except to
warm my hands by rubbing them together
near that same lamplight, while the fishermen

trudge past laden, with a greeting for me –

    Also, if it comes to that,
our better judgment speaks in many voices.

    Far reaching, the ideals we have gathered up on
shingled beaches, where the lone wolf strides,
one ear to the wave, the other half-cocked,

never too adamant when it comes to
a hesitation, maybe, for the weather's sake;
an interruption, to scare the geese up,

or a bony meal gleaned from dried dung.

Oh, I am not persuaded by the spear thrust
deep into the side of existence, nor will my sweat roll
in sweeter drops from anguished strangers' faces,

but I can tell you this:

all nourishment derived from the hibiscus
must fragrant seem as fragrant be,
even while the law gainsays
or the peach should lose its tactile quality:

therefore:

be holy when holiness suits,
crimping no one's style thereby.

Ask directions to the nearest cratered terrain,
that sheep may safely graze, not step on mines,
due to an expert's learned, probed opinions.

Cast out the foreign armies. Blindly rush
to their destruction, not to yours, my boy,
with your cap twisted tightly between your knees
and a look of abandonment where a smile should rule.

Test and be tested, but respect
your neighbour's banties.

Cool your heels on rent-a-dune,
fly hunchbacked over hills on fire
where crops should thrive, of wheat and maze,
and steep your gaze in the beauty of destruction

    while you cannot help it.

    But then help it!

    The august moon, the chirping finch,
the blades of grass, the seed-heads training
their fashioned perfection there where the playful wind
spills what they felt as burdens once or twice
    but mostly held in reserve for this moment.

The gorse pods crack and mean the same.
The campfire's black interior smokes,
the children search for pebbles, to catapult
    bottles to smithereens – meaning the same.

    A crafty devil squats on my heart's doorstep,
smoking cheroots, glancing towards my hearth,
    where maybe he anticipates some comfort.

    Let me be kind to every visitor, but firm,
and not a bit behind when it comes to insisting
on rudiments, such as dress. Let me not be

crude or unbending, though my breath come short
or hot sun scorch my back's flayed skin, and

let me perhaps simply return to my meal,
without being able to justify my lack of hospitality,

    since every man's triumph reflects his sin
    and no man should invite bold devils in.

*

231

The earth objects to the spirit's knife
but when the right man steps up close
we need not wonder at the black bird's flight,
nor should the hand on the railing
make us shake with apprehension.

This much is clear, that our own temporary
wasteful existence in the garden,
beneath the pear tree from which once
a cross was fashioned to blur life's outline,
offers no scope to the blind swine.

But I fear the cataract down into doubt,
and the risk inauthentically taken I deplore,
even as my nature cries out to right wrongs,
both of the fire and of the blood, distinguished
another time on the steps to the tomb.

Eventually the reeds choke the sky from view,
down comes the axe, heads roll, bodies
are wrapped once more in film of weeds
while red-winged blackbirds sound like bells,
silver bells, perpetually clinging to the reeds.

People forget we have power to dwell in thought
on what they in their grief have left to chance
and the questions they ask, the gestures they make
instruct us – or extinguish what we feel
depending on the way our nature leans.

And the personal commitment, the prior
roots our terror-deploying faculties have sunk,
the logic we've desired to accept like sap,
speaks volumes, perfects dreams, overjoys
our reborn self, to become of deeds the vanguard.

Their scandal must not shake us, but instead
move mountains away, whose bulk has intervened
to make death seem troublesome, the rough retreat
open in the past to all members of the family
but suddenly twice removed, as in a play.

Why has energy run the gamut of life's stages
but never once yet stopped itself before the wall,
by good will built, tradition's stone by stone,
with sacrifice the mortar – why not say it –
and the father's eye awaiting the final beginning?

* *

232

Give me time to disentangle from before the mind's eye
    the issue of a thousand days.

On these marshes disembodied identities still float
and where generals once betrayed Caesars and
    Caesar's Jupiter, relaxed backwards against a wall,
pale images now seek in reverence the just tie.

    Around the pool stand the vexatious sisters
deploring, hand on chin, the absence of reflection.
    Nevertheless bathe in the cold, unfriendly water,
over the crown, the imagined ministers dipping you down.

    I am cold and the world rejoices in my splendour.
    I have wished freely to interpret the order of days.
The twin pools of my eyes must bathe the world's conception.

    For he who sends me speaks another tongue
    and his shoes are symbols for the world's transgression.

Why may I not fix my destiny as the tailor the
eye of the needle before inserting the thread?
What great mystery still prevents me from
overstepping the righteous limits imposed upon
the creation of my little finger?

I am exact in my duty, slow to give vent to rancour
and passion's children may in air dance out
the configurations of an implacable night sky – we refuse
them the rebellious confrontation, us the lust for life,
only up to the point where passion secedes – then
the peacock fans, one explores aurora borealis.

Oh good my Lord, you have sent me.
What might I not have done in the past with the
studied appreciation of this knowledge! And may
all such conversation only serve to set up the table,
the chairs, the room in readiness. Let us wait.

The walk along the seafront where the birds
avoid all contact with the sunlight's origin,
where trees outline the noonday sky
giving the impression of great ease,

has afforded me no angelic thrill,
nor will demons rise to inform my eye
with their incestuous struggles for recognition,
but I propose to make known my profit.

Beneath the horse chestnut trees, covered in ivy,
the stone dwarf sits, awaiting the resurrection,
and we know the he feels the crystals in his marrow,
where pain originates, he feels how they crackle,
dissolve and set, each facet reflecting delusion.

Of course we have moved away from the story now
and we search where the tree trunk has been hollowed
by fungus and by the decisive action of decades;
we search for the ultimate tale, beyond which
neither action nor narrative of action can exist.

Only the one word teaches that the word we seek
was the one given, which we understood inside out.
Therefore between the word given and this word
men move whose delight in death has dwindled
to the single atom designated as recorded time.

You, word, if in my stupor I address you
and make do with the best blood so far achieved,
would nothing else precede – succeed these limits?
Not the hat cocked over the left ear, nor the cigarette
between yellowing teeth? And should I continue?

The turbulence in the city, as I view it from the tower
high above fatigued crowds murmuring concessions,
chanting brief testaments of rebellion and revolution,
begins to be by darkness chewed and swallowed
and naked ladies give their all to the neon lights.

*

I walk on roads and kick stones with my feet
so absolute that they become concrete.

* * *

233

M

She has in my heart made a place
for herself with her stormy ways.
Am I to learn human affection
of the sort that lets not judgment mar
   nor good taste bar
and will my fondness of this real game
   grow and acquire a name?

She has made my mind a considerate thing
versed in the little ways of a love
that searches to accommodate itself
to the tired eye, the unsteady hand.
   The grain of sand
feels noticed in this love she teaches,
   by example shows, not preaches.

For once I wish to invite guests,
although that smacks of foolishness
but I desire the roundabout way,
not speed on busy thoroughfare,
   laden with care's
fresh cargo of some playful jewels,
   the heart's daily renewals.

*

Midnight: I see the late hour out,
surrounded by familiar furniture.
My children's pictures on the walls betoken
a spirit borne to love, not broken.

Some call this life: the trivial round;
unthinking men, with eyes for glamour.
Will they not put the horse before the cart
and learn that life's the end of art?

*

235

We went by car, along paved roads,
between hedges by time unspoiled,
still serving their honourable purpose of
keeping the cows or the sheep confined,

to Crawfordsburn Park, rambling stretches
of beach and meadow, and I can say:
the sea looked less spectacular today,
not so much challenged by the black rock.

Eoin drove, hands firmly on the wheel,
mind set on distribution of favour,
as one who knows, not from without,
these glens, and what their life's about.

Myself, I'm a stranger in these parts,
still grateful for what I'm shown and taught.
I sit in the front seat, safety-belted
practicing the art of careful contentment.

Nor man nor beast may speak in jest
of what the passing heart holds dearest
and the worm gnaws at the ageing bone
to remind me: friend, you're not alone.

But cancel what a rhyme or two suggest.
Mairead and the children in the back,
mostly reflective this time, drew breath
each instant in the knowledge of security,

as vaulting lime and fluffy ash
drew breath too, outside the tin and glass,
rushed past, leaving us undisturbed:
a gate – a glimpse of new-mown grass.

The eyes have much as you leave Newtownards
in any direction, walking or by car,
not counting what archaeologists maintain,
or the stewards of the town's anatomy,

that men's bones may beget men again,
or dragon's teeth, sown centuries ago,
still today sprout as tragic causes,
that mutilate men and usurp their places.

But I'm only a stranger in these parts
and riding to Crawfordsburn in a car
I practice certain more leisurely arts
not fit to take part in this war.

Never mind, I have a heart like others,
the will, sometimes, to fiercely hate,
to see in you only my worst suspicions,
to convict you because you kill the stranger.

* *

236

Lord, give us ways and means for our survival.
The power you take from us, that you once gave,
we tested and abused, of your arrival
unmindful, leaves us merely grace and grave.

But grace will not extend, nor grave transport
and so we burn and freeze, in fire and ice.
We institute, drag men before time's court,
or hope to fail, to prove Christ can't come twice.

In cultured mirrors we obtain some rest
while cities crumble, lawlessness grows chronic,
wisdom is purged and on each heart impressed
the telling cipher: bestial or demonic.

'Perhaps, like children's games, as plays dramatic,
you build my realm – implicit – not hieratic.'

*

237

Pride and honour, honour and pride,
what are they both except straw inside,
and a man's rage builds to burst
to satisfy pride and honour's thirst.

*

238

While the chatter goes on downstairs,
the men on the scaffolding, bemused
    by so much coming and going,
    to-ing and fro-ing,
lay brick by brick all the same,
straighten that line, drop the plumb,
    fit joist to rafter:
    they know what they're after.

The cats on the warehouse roof
    dissolve in laughter.

*

239

Lord, give us ways and means for our existence.
We cannot out here dream your spirit's doing
nor stay with it inside. In your eyes hide
all obvious things, accessible to wooing.

But once we stand with bare feet on plain ground
a fear befalls us and we seek our mother
alone in some strange crowd. We shout out loud
and turn our brains off, looking for some other

revealed, and more mysterious, source of warmth,
as though beyond the earth's clouds lay salvation,
not here within this brain. What your words gain
our passionate efforts spoil, unless occasion

demand from us what we could not have offered
but as spiritual risk: the right hand proffered.

*

240

Mother, in mind's solitary being
clearly the last resort – or at least
hand against forehead in anguish
when the brute realistic decries

all measures wise, when the choice
taken fits nowhere – or let's say
as though your son's gift of digestion
called all food in question.

*

241

Never think of yourself as alone for long

Never think of yourself as alone
for long, or carry the spent life
out before the traps of the age
drive the life into rage.

Settle down on sand while
the tide its carriage refreshes
and use those hours of repose
in delight as the heart grows.

Goodness may swallow a man
and spit him out whole, not
vaguely detached, from sense
snatched, at time's expense.

The idle hours, by comparison
not so withdrawn from love
as some would maintain, might
filter rain through light.

Go, begin the day's work
on time, anger the flesh if
required, speak truths to the
sun before you are tired.

*

242

The madness of children fills the air.
They swat the aeroplanes from the sky,
pull priests and sages by the hair,
and maybe, if the papers don't lie,

> we'll soon see them riding
> on sticks, for the fun of it.
> If anybody asks, say:
> 'They let us have our way'

*

243

The thimble pierced by the needle
concentrates the mind to a point.

Compare to this your longish life.

Would it create a furore
if we left ourselves open, from scratch,
to death's melting moments?

*

244

Prophets laugh their way to heaven;
idle, down to earth they slide.
Crocodiles in bogs go hungry
though their maws be open wide.

*

245

Prophets trip over confessions
discarded on the cobbles by a boy,
but when you announce you have grounds
for discretion, they clap for joy.

*

246

Lords, laugh yourselves through the sun's
spectacular widowhood. Make amends
for an arrow never having pierced a heart.
Draw from the fire the spark
most suited to your brain's abomination.

But never feed wool to a dragon;
that draws fire from its arse.
If you care for health and happiness
keep a clear eye on Mars.

*

247

The doves descend like a spiral stair
down to the ground through outraged air
past wet roofs, glistening slates.

In the damp wood a hunter waits –
leans back against a tree and smiles –
the distant fog his eye beguiles.

*

248

An Intrusion

From the mountain dusk
and why not,
the pillared cloud moves out,
or appears, if you like,
and on it ride,
one leg to each side,
several gods, in easy repose,
smiling from ear to ear.

The perfect illusion of this thing
peels back, reveals
what the cold starlight feels.
But the gods ride on
good purpose in each stride,
each step a mile wide
and they look at one another,
make a sign, feel fine,
turn towards you reading this
and with one sudden gallop
rush into you, are swallowed up.

Your mind becomes a buttercup.

*

249

Hard to Believe!

It couldn't have happened
but it did, in among the
small houses by the track,

that a clown knocked on doors
and begged to be let in
but the people drove him off.

They drove him off because they felt
uneasy in front of that face,
triple-tone magic, rough eyes,

and they rushed to their beds,
some switched on television,
others fell down dead.

The next day, in the newspapers,
would you believe it,
an accident was reported

and under the picture of an
elephant black print said:

   'The Clown is Dead!'

I have an idea this means
we can hope for improvement
along lines of poetic humour.

*

250

An Impertinence

A man sat down,
on his face a frown,
his hat too tight,
eyeglasses, to help his sight.

In his hand he gripped
a pipe. Tight-lipped
he sat and reflected
on the life he protected.

His tired feet
sweated in the heat.
He rubbed his head
and then he said:

I wish I knew
why I feel so blue,
not pink or red,
or maybe white instead.

Not a person heard,
not a single word,
but I know it's true,
because that man was you.

*

251

Power (might, really)

Power's all-embracive thrust
brings gold from sun and moon.
The gold from sun dissolves in dust,
the gold from moon must soon

enhance the child's cry in the crib,
no message carry forth,
but mere complaint, and sore restraint,
from East and South and North.

And we, who in the West fought wars,
reject the power that brought us
to brink of death and madness sad
before an angel caught us.

Therefore keep your power and gold,
stick your sadness up your rear.
If your brains have a shred of life
make your damned selves disappear.

*

252

Crawfordsburn

Out rushes from the storm the sea
waiting to be put right by me.
For theme I choose conversion's soul,
let nagging doubt be my goal,
repair the tissue where it stretched
and have emotion on mind etched.

Out rushes from the sea the storm;
respond to life: respect the norm.
What happens, when we watch our step
and read the bloodstream when we trip?
Nonsense slows down the fighting urge
while glad thoughts the emotions purge.

*

Does a man need to get hit
before he'll slow down a bit,
take stock of the familiar vein
and accommodate himself to pain?

The illusion that we we're birds in flight
seems to make everything alright
until somebody else gets hurt,
and so we fool and fling and flirt.

*

Between the tent pole and the rope
I see the crows on the meadow gather.
Some fling themselves up into the air,
or they throw themselves there, if you'd rather.

Between the rope and the tent pole
a seagull changes its mind
and flies from right to left again,
which is suitable, I find.

*

I don't mean to sound flippant,
my spirit is elsewhere occupied.
Also, the way people behave,
I'll not go to the grave easy
if I'm pushed.

So I propose the following:
You go, I'll stay.

*

I'm surrounded by tents.
The sun shines on my face
and my feet hurt from walking.
Why am I not a king?

* * *

253

The urge to make things fit world,
to ease digestion and brain;
the passion for earth, the willed
struggle to win pleasure from gain;

the bitter cup, sold or resigned,
as the mayfly sparks through fate:
these weigh or inveigh, patterned,
ready with a life to equate.

Nothing has round it but loss
nor breath to extinguish mere flame;
no mere mood from cheap paper cut
locates in itself its name.

No fearfully conceived plan
looks out only on dross;
the stair cannot help but be there,
only forgive what love knows.

Nowhere does danger lurk entire
though the path of growth is clear;
when we arrive we have realized
we could not have left here.

*

254

The time it took from castle to tent
made of our minds a monument
to bold action and natural thought
in clay prefigured, in iron wrought,

and the quick precision we abhor
in terms of saga and folk lore,
the tender mercy, on heaven depending,
some times not quite transcending,

leans in our favour night and day,
crowds out anxiety, fights dismay,
sings its way out of planet's course,
follows flame with finished force,

cracks the wall that holds in seed,
blows the limits minds impede
and first rushes into crown of tree
where frequently you dance with me.

But here on moist ground of turf,
within earshot of the surf,
the pots boil, the pans sizzle
and time plies its testate chisel.

*

6 Lessons

If a rhyme bleeds to death
in the grammatic trap
should the form be adjusted
or is the whole poem crap?

*

It may come down like fire or like sand
but unless it makes bleed
the sun won't set on it
before it goes to seed.

*

We can't hope to make life,
but our love, when it suits,
drinks the blood, feeds us wine,
and our life grows roots.

*

Man, whence your authority,
from the cave or the grave?
Show me the mercy you showed,
the gifts you gave!

*

Look, if it rouses the pity
of the many for the few,
how will glory shine forth,
what will men do?

But the many make matters
worse to threefold.
Therefore pity them
before love grows old.

*

What do you want?
Should I pierce the wall through,
rack the lame dog?
Is anyone home?

If the precepts are right
and god willing,
no satirist spoils us
and windmills keep turning.

* * *

256

Ten Epigrams

I have a hunger that surmounts
and a thirst that drives,
and like any self-respecting cat
at least nine lives.

*

What is it people say?
Long live the king!
and the king never dies – ?
a remarkable thing.

*

Walls and a roof make a house;
the floor hardly matters.
The spirit makes its finest move
when the flesh lies in tatters.

*

Death be gentle, be quick;
make your move on stage.
I'd rather die here now and
take home a living wage.

*

Father, I have sinned;
give me credit for confessing.
I promise to sleep on nails;
it keeps the devil guessing.

*

Come, Squire, find a thing to do;
you're not stretched on the floor prone.
Smash a fist down on the table top;
it's not for nothing you're left alone.

*

The rabbits sprint out of their holes;
the earth's crust trembles.
Who'd want to be stuck underground
while God dissembles?

*

Revolutions mask what hatred
serves up at table.
Freud's couch makes the horse
bolt from the stable.

*

Passion stronger? Or reason?
Such a merry couple they make!
Look how they lead the dance
through downpour and earthquake!

*

The "flux of the modern world"
has heart in it if you look
hard enough, but don't try to capture it
between the pages of a book.

* * *

257

Summation

Heart, are you burnt out?
Never mind the material disarray.
Plunge to the hilt, into the confusion,
the dagger of life's wild sway.

Keep your head down long enough
to avoid the slops pouring out.
Observe the skin on the confusion,
heart, and learn to shout.

*

258

Good Advice

It's easy to make it rain;
only condense the clouds.
Soon you're swimming
on our back among crowds.

Disease and tired eyes
long for pouring rain.
When you've had fun swimming
you start flying again.

You walk, you swim, you fly,
or you sit in the sun.
You were purified by fire,
now that's all done.

So sit down when the sun shines
and don't run or fly.
It only seems like fire
because the flames leap so high.

You know you've been swimming
by the moisture in your eyes.
Now warm yourself by the fire
while the sun inside you shines.

*

259

Lady, when you look at me,
why does guilt creep in your eye?
Why this heavy look of failure –
recalled time gone by?

Do you regret a mistake,
a pleasure half wasted,
half spoiled? Did you
eat more than you tasted?

I did, which is why I
recognize that look, dear.
But my past is cleaned up,
reformed like a book, dear.

So don't fret, don't strain
your conscience, relax
easy into forgiveness,
never mind the axe.

It lops off dead wood,
leaves desire for new growth,
not guilt-ridden half wishing
half dread, to feel 'loath'.

*

260

What the sun rises and sets on
meets me in head and heart.
The wind-still clamouring of rooks
keeps my two hands apart.
All I feel and touch there
thrives as oak, stands as pine
and the wild carnation's scent
bids my spirit recline.

*

261

Does the windmill on the hill
   stand there or not
and does the shadow it casts
   somehow mark the spot
where I once stood
   and reflected whence my name,
and this smouldering fire,
   or the glad sense of shame?

*

262

Work on your patch of earth and sky
until the wheeling stars take hold
and fix the mountain and cloud
in patterns creative and bold.

Then breathe in the flux of stars,
despatch what you know across earth's
trembling face and skilled limbs
and bless all deaths and births.

*

263

The sun piles mountains up in me,
draws clouds back and forth across
my vision where I see and feel
and often beneath this onslaught reel.

But the sun also questions
how or why I behave
and finally, in tune with it,
I let it shine into my grave.

*

264

The sun had been stuffed under a pillow.
Generations slept on it and felt
their dreams warmed and enlightened,
but when they woke they were frightened
and the ice in their hearts would not melt.

Some carried flame to the world's wood,
if that might create a warm soul.
Others hid in caves in the hills
in fear of death by their own wills;
the millions were swallowed by death whole.

Now the sun rides home on a stallion
through woods cursed by the past
over land by mere progress blighted
and it sees all these wrong things righted,
and its light is enlightened at last.

*

265

The Dark Beast in Man

The earth turns round, the sun turns round
and, helpless, I stand by and smile
for surely where the planet roams
the star may hardly rest a while.

Or should I fear the roaring tide
of black space troubling from within,
the logic of these massive laws
whose roots feed where my heart has been?

Does hand reach out and spin the wheel
so that in motion more humane
life's glory may bring peace on earth
and not distress of guilt and pain?

Gold figures feast at table decked
for final guests in wedding gowns.
Dim eyes look up, abhor such sight,
false heart beats fast, impure mouth frowns.

Such thoughts as these impair my sleep
and flatter not my waking hours
for in each man a dark beast lurks
which, unobserved, his life devours.

*

The New Sun

The sun sheds light on all it pleases.
We rearrange our lives like that.
It penetrates and then disguises
in subtleties the surface flat.

Behind the light it sheds, the sun is
not normally what men would think.
There darkness rules with iron rod
a realm as black as printer's ink.

Behave yourself, sun, or be punished.
You dare not instigate bad days.
The scythe you bear as golden emblem
deprives us of our puppets' craze.

The pristine shackles your heat smithied
are not required now that you turn
your face towards men, their loved women
and children you refuse to burn.

I trust you, for it seems you relish,
exemplified as bone and marrow,
heroic comfort and bold laughter
with no harm done to widow's sorrow.

The sun has nothing new to offer
but it neglects old cares and woes.
The light it sheds must meet reflection
and then perception in its throes.

When I was young I trained my eyesight
beneath a bridge near ocean's bay
by staring at the light the sun shed
and risking injury from its ray.

Undoubtedly my eye accepted
the ministrations of the sun.
I stood and gazed, with eyelids widened,
intent on what my brain had won.

I pity those who feel this blaze,
and their soft flesh has not been tested.
Do they not roam on earth's cold loam
with mind and body uninvested?

* *

267

Does my land need the plough?
I have nothing but patience.
The cool brain of the fly,
its memorable conscience,

will do as an antidote
to the more subtle traditions
of a love that would extradite

my opinions of a dark age.
We should take pains to resuscitate,
beginning with the quaint midge
trapped by the spider,

our culture's poor stooge:
earth mother, and feed her
our ambitions and skills.

Unless we manage cruder
shapes when our light falls
on heritage with greater ease,
we see how love extols

the merits of a later phase
of the world than hot Troy
or Rome and its truer ruse.

*

268

Now believe that all is well.
The heightened influence of the dance,
the awareness of the blackbird's call,
danger beyond a child's defence:

these are the world's appeals to love.
In sleep the dreamer's nerves announce
how much strength his heart might give,

how sensitive behind man's eyes
magic hides darkness in its groove
whence seven wonders once arose
to placate the invader sun.

But these high hopes were meant to please
not bring explosion to a pin
or Christ's care into disrepute.

I guess our luck has come and gone.
We are left with daylight and delight,
false memories of an instant moon
no straight line thinker can equate

with moods where souls may intervene
to dream of space no mind may fill –
so spurious are we, and profane.

*

269

Oh do not tamper with the root.

Do we not own the brightest star
and have no cause to play the reed?

Within the heart dull cravings stir,
reach out for where a weakness lurks
to teach us envy and esteem.

The terror of an idle lark
before it climbs to make the sky
its whole home where no strange eyes look
would have the songbird swift and shy.

But nature has it: we must choose,
here hearts that bleed, there eyes that shine,
that somehow we too become just,
particles in a sightless stream,
too loyal to avoid love's chase.

Our eyes take in that reddish streak
left by some passing god on clouds,
some god too consequent to strike
a mortal heart that might collide
with dreams too elegant to ride
past mountains not too high to climb.

*

270

Beside the stream the willows burn
luminous in yellow light.

The red sun sets behind the barn.

Faintly from the shack the lute
announces the approaching storm,
entering the sky so late
that with each god-forsaking strum
angry clouds are pitched about.

What is this willow-darkening stream,
making my star's light abate
and leaving but an empty husk
dancing where the walls abut
on gardens set in windless hush,
patient for an artless moon?

The earth's excitement looms so huge
there on those great pines I mean,
profoundly marking out the life,
careful to explore our mind.

Some men prefer experience live,
gathering when the nuts turn brown
and stored as honeycomb of love.

*

271

I'd rather not discuss it, friend,
how sometimes, in a darkened room,
among the god-forsaken crowds,
I stand and feel my heart grow old,
so far removed from kindred minds.

I'd rather not accept the truth
that these are not the golden years
reserved for you and me, my friend,
to walk in step among the trees
and speak of what our hearts know best.

Therefore I spend my idle hours
alone and burdened with regret
that you, my friend, and I, your friend
are cast by this enduring light
into an everlasting shade.

But never mind, our tired eyes
have seen these visions once before
and then we cloaked ourselves in spite
and offered up the world to hate
as though no merit lay in truth.

*

The vast majority of people in England
    live in houses built of brick.
My brother George moved into a tower
    on a hill overlooking the moors.
The local population suspects him of
    demon worship and sorcery.
One Thursday morning he came face to face
    with the devil on a horse.
He decided he was ready for a contest
    and challenged the devil by voice.
We found pieces of George hanging from
    the trees near a black crater.
People visit this place once a year now
    sacrificing their children before a shrine.
I cannot accept responsibility for George
    because he hated me and cursed me.
I can never return to England now, because
    people point at me there and say:
Return to the darkness! Return to the darkness!
    Show us the way into the Night.

*

273

Avoid detection by
courting the commonplace.

Among the sanctified hills,
hung with garlands,
observe the slaughter of the innocents.

I am protected, but
my flesh suffers pain.

*

Borrow money from slaves
but do not drink their water.

When you ride on the waterwheel
and the children applaud your singing
pretend you have not heard.

Then carry the severed head
of the daemon to the grave.

*

Would you rather probe the heart
than carry the study of life forward?

Those who have made contact with the life
and their cares leave them neither rest nor hope,
how do they avoid the gratitude of the oxen?

I am young and straight in limb
but my eye was long darkened.

* * *

274

I am not content to live here
among reflections of an intemperate moon.
  My house leans against the hill

  and the maidens surround my deathbed,
courting dateless disasters and false hopes,
storing in purple sheets their purple agonies,

  and I hinder the locusts, the mice;
  thistle and convolvulus:
  vermin and weeds, from participation.

Do the failures of my ancestors bar the sky?
Or would colour in my child's cheeks put me
  in mind of my own insolent years?

Now what counts is the happy correlation of
  matter and feeling, cool leaves laid
on wounds gained in the service of Society.

*

275

  Yes, you have observed
  how the cruel heart makes stone flakes
chip off the surface of china cups lifted
  promiscuously to an inelegant mouth,
    while lips over red teeth
  and the magnitude of saddened eyes,
as though a clown had dealt this hand before,
  personifies the realm of beasts, or
    tenderly advises men to pray.

*

276

two smiles

The full moon hangs on the fence
and beyond, where the tourists roam,
drawing barges laden with nectarines,
blends of tea, cheese and sausages,
the old emperor surveys the Nile.

An image of the moon hangs on the fence.
Beyond this fence, where the tourists roam,
the old emperor surveys the Nile:
the barges, laden with nectarines,
with blended tea, cheese and sausages.

*

277

The PLO has left Beirut but
first they filled the air with lead.
I guard against sarcastic speech
and aim to practice what I preach.

*

278

No one may exemplify
the rack of pain driving
light out of mind
and the night arriving.

*

279

When all our structures fail
and the beast eats the poor man
we may build on that land
which barbarians once overran.

Our new buildings must sit
with their walls buttressed within
and we need make no provision
against the anger of our kin.

The elements prove our rest,
tiling the cosmic roof,
and the god we invite
shall not lack for proof.

Let all of earth shake
or arrogance tempt the mind,
while rhetoric snuffs candles
we must try to cure the blind.

As we strain to express life
and the art we practice grows,
let us hand in our claims sheets
for the full promise god owes.

*

280

We are not allowed to disport ourselves
as though an angry mob howled within.
The miraculous properties of contentiousness
must be questioned, even late into the night.

*

281

Come, cease from stabbing at old wounds.
Look around you, make new friends and
lay yourself open to the energies of the fountain,
not omitting the cold eye, of course.

*

282

Why should it suddenly seem such an imposition
that the carefully laid plans of past generations
provoke laughter, at the market and in the stable,
while an imaginary host of troubled wayfarers
consciously involves itself in pagan observancies?

*

283

Oh you who are the source of words
and not in competition with my joy,
if my vision contained your reward
and death a multitude of choices,

would freedom in the world look less wide
and my fettered spirit refuse to chide?

Ambitions leave a trail of want and woe
so that the daylight may be propertied.
The magic film our eyes renew
prevent the tree from prospering.

The quick earth our eyes replenish,
the bits of sky our heart's thoughts rescue,
stand in the will of life replete
with treasure, gold in iron cask.

Techniques you practiced, trade you plied,
feeling and thought in bold words cast,

continue, in spite of love, to implicate
the slavering vixens, the malignant sisterhood,
unless we think of Christ returned innate
in science, not there because he should.

*

284

When I examine my near life's end,
the removal of love from under the yew
out into the spirit, where it may stand
eternal and unexplained, fit to draw
breath on earth's unadulterated ground,

I realize that these stout limbs must forego
all truth told to associate or remind,
the lack of shadow borne out by the firefly,
bloody judgment of the lamb grown mordant,
equally the loose shift of the passerby.

Let me instead hoard fruitful precepts
and the market's produce without delay,
rich pleasures, not picked with forceps
but adamant virtue's generous outlay
and the goodly lie to popular deceits.

The eager trials by huge men highlight
what moves among the stars as faults.
   Oh anxious fingers without lute!
   Existence stripped of every rite –
and action as no more than dream's prelude – .

*

285

Why do the clouds, like a city, weigh me down?
But the rising sun holds heavenly hope for me
and as trees blossom pink throughout the orchard
my eagle rises and circles over the hare.

In another country trains speed through tunnels,
break records, pile carriages against the embankment,
or dump their make-shift loads into the sea.
Here sit the smoking gentlemen in easy chairs.

The bubbling waters of the hot spring near me
are filled with bodies basking in the limelight.
Night descends as the vines droop gracefully
to shield my body from the cold starlight,

*

286

A hostile fish with razor teeth
eats its way into my shoulder.
Planet scrapes against planet,
marrow heals within bone.

In the observatory the lovers weep:
matchsticks, dead for the lack of friction

*

287

Where darkness is forced out by light
and makes the nether regions bright,
exploring what the eye may hold
there spent beneath the icy cold,

where stars in inky skylight dance
and gradually dawn removes the veil
from East to West, let man be blest,
and cast his pain out without fail,

there diamond, as the hard heart's prize,
is rent from coalface otherwise
than nine to five man would confess
and sleep through dawn in wantonness.

*

288

The reborn intellect must hew
a new path through from me to you
and where contentment still holds sway
there wayward wood is worn away.

*

289

Let existence be food for this thought,
not old wine to new wineskins brought;
arm the brain for incessant strife
that it may win its rest for life.

*

290

I am no murdering fool
impressed by the white man's burden,
the black man's attitude's and chants:
I would remove from eyes the trance

from titular respect the feather
and sail my ship in any weather.

*

291

This intellect cannot tire,
it sleeps where people tread
and never aims higher
than what its master said.

It slips beneath the curtain
and stoops to conquer best
where love has torn its raiment
and poor truth stands undressed.

It gains by losing face
and magic must endure
until by hook or crook
faint heart comes pure.

*

292

You know existence by its smell,
its memory makes the spine cord flinch
and where you touch it, good my son,
its reflex makes your slipper pinch.

So set out to surprise the beast
before it grips you by the scruff
and kicks you where you like it least
and makes you scream: Enough! Enough!

*

293

If it leads to trouble
and the sweat breaks out on your brow.
Perform in the circus –
Look! You are doing it now.

*

294

Somewhere out there
lighthouses exact tribute
from ships not shaped for sailing.

Somewhere out there
pine trees stand, uninfluenced
by the world's meagreness.

Social causes captivate people
and eat them. I hate myself meanwhile
for the tenderness in my bones.

*

295

But where do the flocks of birds alight
when the boundless sea foams up into eternity?
How shall I attach myself to live
once the meadows have been ploughed?

Perplexed I operate my flesh
according to directives from on high
beneath the scalp, where fierce birds of prey
work angular beaks into grey matter.

*

296

Sadly I make no impression on anyone
but the gestures of melancholy are what counts
   and I would sell my birthright,
     honestly,
if anything better came along.

The popular reproaches give me some pain
and no man knows better than I what work means
for I have captured my soul in a butterfly net
and the vast institutions of the universe
   according to elaborate plan
     give sanction,
     as usual,
   to everything under the sun;
as long as the doctor's house calls come under the
   National Health.

Bring along your binoculars when you visit the park
because the distances today have become unmanageable.

The deer criss-cross the road every which way and
my father has pronounced on one more point of certainty.

While the butcher locates his cleaver
I have an announcement to make:

But sadly I make no impression on anyone.

*

297

Are people not more wonderful today
than they ever were, and yet we know
no more about them than is written
or painted, or scratched into metal.

People have mouths for speaking
and their tribal patterns incite
hatred among equals, bad feeling
and an everlasting concern for money.

How will earth be populated when
the scratches in the metal fester
and too many birds have no place to
roost or nest, or to raise fledglings?

Dry-eyed we stare into space, make
allowances for tables and chairs,
adjust our mental attitudes and give
some sign to prepare for communication.

People have our welfare at heart
and the forests they transport us through
lie so long open under the stars until
an able-bodied man performs the operation.

Then, if only for a day, perhaps longer,
the knitting stops in the living room,
the cattle raise their heads on the meadow,
the digestion of the truth leaves no testimony.

I am not one to give people credit
for agonies they accept, for the quicker
dance around the maypole when leisure
would suffice, but my conscience cringes.

This fact leaves me breathless at times
because when answers are required of me
to questions I cannot recognize, my
brain leaves me desperately in the lurch.

Why have I, poor puppet with a cough,
not the gift of the cutting remark, the
prompt retort to set the record straight,
once challenged by the passionate judge?

But I begin to contemplate and dream,
unwilling to set my heart in motion
for the sake of an intemperate enjoinment,
transfixed by the subtlety of cut leaves.

Beguilement of the more physical extremes
means my glad task, my fast confusion
at the street corner, linked into Christ's
arm, waiting for the light to change.

* *

298

Mother

Mother, may sweet contentment from thee flow
that I may not, in my extremity, intemperate grow
but turn, compelled by no more than the desire
to be in your beauty, to warm by your fire.

I am advised, by men of an age long past,
that those who simply yield prosper at last
while men who would set bold face against a sky
displease your heart and life passes them by.

You are by nature promised, nature at rest,
drawn from tears, sweet truth at mother's breast,
smallness miraculous, pearl restrained from pain,
handed across, not down, perfect and plain.

Mother, I drink complete peace from your eyes
not to feel tranquil, but to become more wise.

*

299

The longing to be employed stems
from the need for effect and cause,
not from fear of nature's whims.
If you wish life were otherwise
when the state of a black mood becalms
your spirit and soon overlays
your heart with hopes of better climes,

let living daylight imbue
your eye, as your memory Athens and Rome,
and make will towards love defray
the cost of existence spent in dream.
No need for temperament to prolong
the pain, when body might run free
on meadows, and the brain sing.

A judgment makes our skin believe
every which way, and limbs fling
cares to the wind that we might grieve
in style to make bells ring,
not madly scrape and blindly grope
within earth's elemental offering
trapped in vengeance, in an historic groove.

*

300

It's enough to make a move towards peace
in a country where strife is the norm.
Even a kind word breaks the ice.

Don't depend on personal charm
to help you conquer the abuse
levelled at every effort of reform.

Virtue cannot succeed like vice.
Hold out before the moral refrain,
dig in behind some obvious cause.

Then, when the streets, filled with refuse,
and packs of dogs on the loose,
leave the sovereign mind without base,

the adulterous tongue with no excuse,
your secret life may look bad
in newspapers, as popular exercise.

But criticism only baits the bigot.
World and art enjoy interplay
in dead men's spiritual ragout.

Yóu keep fit to stake property out
and emulate the name of a prudent man,
nót puffed up with a confident air.

*

301

To keep art free of the world
is a major concern of mine.
Whatever structure we build
should hold in the light of the moon
but must stand in the sun's field.

Then art submitted to the world
will incline man to his example
and leave his righteous flags furled
that his life may remain as simple
as the truth that makes evil yield.

*

302

A glance back

I was not much past twenty when I took my flight,
    dreams and visions shortened my days.
From one day to the next I expected the world's end.

Most men who saw me pass closed their doors,
    kept out the strange faceless energy,
but some had read well in the book of foreshadowing.

The visions I saw comforted my waking hours
    surrounded my breath with the scent of spectacle.
At night I slept in strange houses or under trees.

How the earth reached out with cold arms for me!
    Those were the terrible days of frustration
when the fires of anxiety gradually licked me clean.

*

303

Why does the sun encourage me to
drink death and speak violence?
The moods I work out in myself
terrify the population, and I
prefer the immensities of space.

In my heart the loneliness drives
hard bargains with my blood.
My brain has lost scope and would
rid my mind of its weaknesses
while enchantment covers my eyes.

Oh good Samaritan, at the spring
no fountain develops, no guest
shakes the host's hand gratefully.
My hand trembles, therefore these
leaves wilt, fresh from the bud.

A glad isolation of the will finally
descends like fog into the hollow of
love's passion, twines tendrils around
the blond arm, while music nearby
pretends that the trees are liquid.

*

304

It makes such a wonderful noise, this
double standard of fruit and flower
when the casual deaths along the track,
looped into an ever ready confusion,
bleed white as lily petals, though
not obscurely, my friend.

Oh good people, leave these things,
they have nothing to contribute to life
and their dust settles into grooves.
Speak in a lowly voice of love, not
wrapped into soiled sheets, set
up on counters for sale.

*

305

I am not at home in these hills, where lions
roar out their messages, meaning an endlessness.
I would rather sit still where the trees shade
in immense shadow the wind's immensity.

I would rather clasp in loving embrace these
perfect impressions upon an evening's candour
but my manacled shape trips over roots and
loosely defines itself without effecting an entry.

*

306

Come sleep with me beside my side
and let your beauty grace my bed
and perfectly betray me here
with secrets fit for no man's head,

that by the morning we may find
the issue of the age to come
or nothing that makes tragic news
for children of the deaf and dumb.

*

Beauty

Only the illuminations of bygone days,
unfolded within the eye's protective circle,
may create, as worked remnants of peace,
(as inclusions where the shark rips)
the pallid objects of a sleepy love.

Never perform for the few
what the many since Noah's flood knew.
But you may, if you like,
please the unhappy figure there
seated between the moon's knees.

You may too, while the town still stands,
mix imagination in beauty's bowl
and bake a mess of fine goods
calculated to reck and to record
the able hand's quiet dispassion.

Would I not rather move among crowds,
you say, smiling behind that hand,
and perhaps trade in insufferable agonies
and ritual moods, and periods of mankind,
since so much depends on that today?

Even the cruel magic of a
government devised of scraps,
minuscule tendencies puffed up for viewing,
ought to be held below water's rim
where angels speak softly.

I could locate, if I meant such ease
or flew into passion directly on contact,
forms too beautiful for us
and the mellow buttercup on the hot land
would assume the perfection of glass.

Would such an equality of views
merit a mention in the national news?
The spiked thistle, patterned trope,
truly inflexible before the gaze,
slants in direction of light biological.

Adorning purpose of metal sky,
exposed crystal on the wintry pane,
moment of carnal insight past invective:
these motivate the plastic surgeon's hand
or cultivate a style in excitement.

Floor, walls and ceiling sound hollow
unless an energetic dream may follow
hot on the heels of past experience viewed
in retrospect, contract of hindsight renewed
in some legitimate bond of our history.

Purely imagined, the violence we fear,
not the poor aspects of death we picture,
as reflection in itself only half faced,
entertains the bluebell, is repulsed
by thistledown drifting on smooth air.

Consequence in the hazelnut's shell
requires leadership, mastery of self.
Perpetuity on mossy incline
lugubriously rants. The particular shift
of red towards white makes stardust drift.

Why I am not incarcerated in the world
or in a manufactured likeness of it,
let those decide who mirror love
prior to its consummation, and then neglect
the vast indifference flooding the mind.

Beauty can make ideas come to life.
The faculty which tenderly adheres to fact,
willing to wait until the shell is cracked,
gives itself time too, for renewed birth,
conquest of bitter triumph and loss.

The latitude we give to those who stretch
the detailed ministration of our hope
beyond passion's point, affords us too
a vigour we could never destroy
by practical extreme or supererogation.

Then that's the sea we need to navigate,
all men alike, women and children first,
harboured in our interest, our mute concern,
not sacrificed to an intolerant purity
no god could match in his right mind.

Or the laughter we sometimes feel
cosseting the face with paternal hands
as half explicit roots where the finch
flits through between the pine tree's twigs
and nestles to absorb the sun's warmth –

There are – these are – trivial finds,
such as let fledglings grow strong.
Some callers, educated brains, would
rather insist than nurture into light,
kindle and coax, make acceptable.

But freely gains who freely gives,
according to his kind of measurement,
his manner of treatment, technique of
meting out, be it judgment or kiss,
crude structure couched in tenderness.

For we have available, at freedom's cost,
a nuclear blast, the cheering population
prior to the blast, afterwards the sure
knowledge of some heroics wasted
where flavour of love went untasted.

Substance called beauty always is.
This thought no sentiment may erase
nor mood make glitter as cold steel
because of what materialists feel,
realists pander to, idealists engross.

Beauty can not be shaken or removed.
It may not lend itself to the bastard control
at all times, poor wights, sarcastically speaking,
nor turn on sexual exploits for a second,
but you'll not name a thing it deplores.

We do the castigating, the dressing down,
not the image we've allowed to impress us
with some final power, remarkable characteristic,
because I hurt a little or sleep in,
as though that could create a barrier.

Belief makes beauty what it seems:
riders under a night sky; gladioli
in rows by a grave; summoned ghosts,
cool in their appreciation of our effort;
a swineherd on his way to mass.

But all of these would avoid the taint
of that secondary source, emission from which
would rule us towards some other-worldly plane
where thirst is not quenched but temporized,
hunger not stilled but rendered void.

What shall we call it: the mysitific urge?
The bane in all Poetic and Rhetoric?
The classification of the body politic
under rubrics we struggle to maintain
when they would maintain us without fuss?

Would beauty then be matter for the process
of life itself, shingled or thatched, or scaled
for passage through water, feathered to lend
an air of grace to those who would breathe
grace itself, under impetuous canopy?

If the picture won't leap into view
why not let the magnitude work on you?
If the brainchild of two thousand years
prefers the pulpit to the living room,
why should a king disturb his ways?

The lassitude I carry from bed to bed,
cot to carnal extinction, terminates
in beauty too, leaves no fatal residue,
though the senses would make the odd addition:
a corner stone here, a wedge block there.

*

The factory girls in the town square,
beneath the town hall, hold their demonstration;
they signal their unwillingness to labour
for passing good at passing wage –
they emphasize this fact by shouting.

Meanwhile the market draws a goodly crowd.
Policemen search bags for hidden weapons,
smoke from chimneys broken by frost
veils the sky, and the tower in the west
excuses the absence of so many Greek ships.

Meanwhile envy disports itself in stone,
the magicians meet to exchange council,
the Lady Hackbut reins in on the parking lot,
unfolds arms and legs, collects bags
and ignores the local stone-age yokels.

Usury complies with expedient policy,
tries a new loophole to avoid a new slump
and wishes it could take up gardening.
But the effortless mile by mile approach of
the future cancels out such ambition.

Me they have set out on the dry land,
forced sticks between my lids, flayed
my skin, left me with nothing to eat but
my heart's contents, apparently poisoned
and nowhere else in demand but here.

Sail past, great ship of destruction.
Drag your tail past my tent, serpent,
I keep my eyes down, my intention clear,
expecting the disappointment any moment
when the beetle becomes the totem of my bribe.

'Carrion comfort' one called this dish
and I'd light his pipe if manners required.
Glory requires a kind of commitment
to test and trial, to see who can lure
best mercy, faith and right judgment.

Our existence demands a type of challenge.
We live shrouded in glory, granted,
like magnificent fish through iced foam,
our eye round to take all beauty in,
our god an enticement to good love.

Remember to breathe in grace, the world's
affluence, tenderly crucified, remember.
Shortcomings lead to nerve refinement,
pain welcomes its master gladly, but
translate, search for the tongue's heart.

At the same time practice the heart's tongue
according to what existence offers, not on
purpose contrary to rules and regulations
but neither thwarting the joy of rebirth:
wickedness instead, the joy of survival.

Did Paul not speak in such-like enthusiasm,
praising in foolishness to thwart the foolish,
mentioning the chain buckled to his flesh
to make the high vision eventually useful,
guarding against flight into abnormality?

He knew the norm, had seen it speak.
Also he had dreamt, proportionately,
a whole set of circumstances, dispassionately,
and later, when the scales dropped, he flew
to the assistance of communities on trial.

Why should any man, technically speaking,
behave differently, given the ways and means
of particular humanity? Are we not blind
first, surrounded by initial misunderstanding,
then approached at last by some catastrophe?

The pain, the humiliation, the disunity
stick in our craw, require some urging
from without, I think, oh hard philosophy!
and while I mean to digest some nihility,
I'll not curse the author who allowed it.

Fish in flight, red-throated diver: these
denizens shrug off ideal definition.
I would claim ownership, if I could,
but the simple variations there prevent me
from rising out of my own depth, scathed.

*

Why should the need for goodness weigh
so heavy on the unperjured conscience?
I create in myself an imbecility
to make room for wisdom, time for love,
and still the need for goodness presses.

Given: the desire to rant and rave,
to leap to the window out of curiosity
or to sit in a futile admission of weak
helplessness, waiting to be boxed
around the ears, for nothing, if you please.

Given also: a readiness to die, to gloat
on the scaffold, oh dear, I could go on,
mention the nail marks in the palms
caused by too virile an intensity;
refer to a shameful shamelessness.

But let's not overindulge in mortality.
The right chemicals, prescribed, help us cut back
on intake here, correlate job and wish,
assimilate self-image and true wit
forced by experience – cure, in short.

It's mother earth we have to thank for that.
Laugh all you like, she'll twist you yet
out of countenance to teach compliance
with mother wit, what you'd know, rule of
thumb – and a jog down the dirt track.

Formal education, by comparison, ends up
ninety per cent circumstantial, a buffer zone
for when your own demon won't leave you alone
but shouts your name out in bad company
and then lifts the embargo on good manners.

My most plentiful supply of action-packed
idiocies derives from a closed-door policy,
energetic and all, with respect to poor relations
and disrespect to the right. I scream with
venom, bite hands when they feed me.

You too can understand this. We live in a
moribund society, conscience beflecked,
the smoky tripod not in use or all too much,
ignorant of authority except the individual whip
and a myriad careers open to the impecunious.

Wilful murder has become the fashion and
the ability to see what is meant by this has
never lacked more light. One attempts
'transvestiture' in art, versatility in science
and periodically I forget my own name.

By stomach, for example, what do you imply?
Like heart, that you have or break? Organic
evolution has split open the trope's womb,
spilled the bowels symbolic, cut off beauty's
legs, trailed brain by the hair through muck.

The categories that have mattered since Kant
have sown shut with catgut love's vagina.
On crude pedestal the hooded apteryx stood,
self-inflicting liver wounds, while the mob
excited itself, mistaking friction for fire.

Themes will run riot before the last bell tolls
spilling its unsound quanta into air
that reeks with acid. Themes such as
love, progress, beauty, economics, truth
take power to handle, glory to fulfil.

*

What the moon makes, the sun undoes
and all is treatment for that higher purpose,
that gentlemen's club with no entrance requirements,
all miracle with touch and property
and inward peace, for the saint's arrival.

If I could abstract from the lofty peaks
the criminal vestiges of classless cloud,
performed in amusement before a fountain,
none of these ghosts would know my name
and the tourists would choose some other climate.

I am inconsequent, I know, my shoes pinch,
the doorbell rings beyond me, I fling
wrong attitudes at right masks; generosity
interests me to a fault, enthrals my nerve,
greatness eats itself into my roots.

The next time an invention intrigues me
I will cut my eye on the stem of a flower.
The next time a horse moves under me,
given the sun rises, the moon falls,
I shall carry my head proudly.

So soothingly the hand the wheat field strokes
yet crows erupt. Dull midwives speak
of mothers dead at childbirth, babes
untoward when the first light shone
into eyes not vested by a rich past.

Gold, livid fruit of enterprise, whetted
appetite prostrate at the feet of mercy,
but skill meticulous as sheets of ice,
freezes the taste out, for what ails man,
and penetrates the side of god with poison.

By collision with sound we learn to hear
and cornered paths teach us to think
forward, on pebbles as on paper.
We fellow lordlings rest on soul
our mead-filled heads, our sensile skin.

Naked anxiety deranges our civilization
and yet, as toad, high-noon charisma
flirts on the stage with purple blood.
The broad beams in the cottage ceiling
are cracked. The iron hooks are rusted.

For the composition of a contemporary life
take mossy cushions under lime green trees,
let mushrooms sprout from hollow logs,
date the event of procreation and then
stand perplexed: you've done nothing yet.

Continue, past the sawmill, where the screams
of parted logs fill air and countryside,
(a recall from my youth in Canada)
huge lorries lumber across deserted terrain,
whistles blow – the splash of corpses into water.

Still nothing. Now some activity builds
just east of the spleen, where the north star
commands the night, pushes in the forehead,
(a recall from earlier forms of literature)
so perceptible that no one seems to notice.

A flood of stars, enticed by too much light,
confronts the prophet, prostrate in his tomb.
Cruelly the marble shudders on his bones.
A wide winged bird floats down and lifts
the stone away. The pale corpse shifts.

Help me here be the master of my moods,
astride each crisis as its crest appears.
Let me not be short-changed by this religion
which labels spirits, keeps time in a box
and allocates eternity to never-never land.

Don't think I don't notice the frost settling
perniciously into the spaces between the cells
on whose decomposition my body depends,
since the break-down of matter precedes
all conquest of doubt, bane of creation.

There, clear-eyed on a grassy plane, in wind
purely uplifted, but not yet eager to fly,
the mere child coaxes joy from cool contact
with stone and tree trunk, blade of grass,
umbel of scented white foam, flower in face.

I have no hearth to sit by and contemplate
the various wishful states of our civilization
but at night some god deposits in my brain
such useful sense as may profit the population
if it but sees – and there's a fable connected.

Under an implemented sky awash with machinery
some boldness still holds some men out to a fate,
ready to snatch them back if the rain threatens,
or mother calls, or the neighbour's gossip
hangs hellfire; and love bargains for contentment.

Be not like those who exercise their wits
only to tickle; make curious moves run true,
true moves run deep, deep purpose stick.
It would quench a dead man's thirst, this wit,
and make of god a casual acquaintance.

Of course we rivet the world's attention
as readily to itself as to things of beauty
but cheerless men despoil their heritage.
We crane our necks beyond past ventures
and wish for stimulus even in the darkness.

*

Locate the source of love's exaggeration.
It may curdle the blood, to speak these words,
but works in void of mute antipathy,
imagined near the threshold of externality,
bargain for strength with the muscle of antiquity.

Bygone ages, thrills and spills of life
compacted when the archaeologist reads,
bounce into bone, fact out of artefact,
can clear the poisoned eye of 'thing-rejection'.
Antiquity stems from shares such as these.

And it rolls the blinds down on modernity
to see such fashioned art as cleaves
to forgone conclusions, though at a price,
since nothing exceeds like success
and even a false system quietens our hormones.

Therefore have no traffic with slayers of mice,
with carbon-copied, candelabra-swinging
habitués of the sacerdotal pyramid.
They actuate without attending to the heart.
Their limp bodies flap in the wind.

If you must breathe excitement into god,
never let on. The performance has to continue
as though men could live under water, like fish,
black, staring eyes to deflect space,
scales to confuse the gaze in vision.

Some tightrope, this. Help where help counts,
injected into veins and arteries at once.
My eye maintains the brimming fix on angels.
My hand roams beneath universal skirts
to differentiate the sexes – not so easy nowadays.

The partridge falls, drowsy, from the pear tree
into a basket held by virgins in khaki.
An element of secular restraint appears in this,
for an hour or so, for those with the inclination
to bathe in limelight while the monkeys frisk.

Monkeys outlive their usefulness, you see.
They imitate old age, with a vengeance.
I make my peace with all these gay illusions
so that no one can fling me, with a smile,
on the scrapheap I prepared during my winter.

When Alice drew the looking glass around her
after the bath, and tiptoed to the window
where lay, spread out, the derelict town,
smoking to bring its energy to the boil,
she voiced, beneath her breath, a malediction.

But Alice had been raised by unsound parents.
Bad weather had prevented her education,
the schooling of incarcerated drives,
so no one should make her responsible for words,
those strange sounds made by voice, lips, teeth and tongue.

Words have a way of punishing Alice.
She never intends the ones she says,
and those she intends have the nasty habit
of curling round and biting into her flesh
no matter how far she holds them out by the tail.

When imagination threatens to surround us
like some primordial cosmic, bird's egg shell,
and the way we drift inside it makes no sense
because our senses have overcome gravity,
accidentally, it's time to watch the heart.

This is the only legitimate form of criticism.
The heart shoots its satellites into brainspace,
its submarines cruise through blood and lymph,
the eye maintains radio contact with the heart,
and all this traffic would be carefully screened.

So soberly I bend over my neat map
to study curves and outlines of mountain ranges,
courses of rivers, liquid metaphors,
where the cool girls laugh and splash
and the boys swing out on ropes and drop.

Here the cave opens towards the blue lake.
I would drive out these foreign serving wenches
who cast a shadow too long for deciphering.
I would give them short shrift, if I knew
how far a man may be guided by his ego.

The blue lake deepens to middle ice
where the Nereids quickly soothe my brow.
I am not settled long before they entertain
their queen and mine, on early television.
Then an abundance of light cleanses me.

* * *

308

I have turned myself inside out.
The operation cost me no money.
Now until death I feast
on milk and honey.

On mild and honey I feast
though unsound men chide me.
Oh mercy of god, stay
lest my good deeds hide me.

*

309

The city stands contrite in stone,
impressed by fact beneath the rain,
unhurried by events so blind
their history makes the clock go round.

The valiant men who built these piles
rest now like diamonds lost in coal
and their ancestors sleep their fill.

Look, heart, you have example here,
achievements of the mind for hire,
and if you like, this city whore
will drag you through the streets by the hair.

Your name, of course, would be protected
and the wounds of pride you have inflicted
would not heal, but remain contracted.

Or, reconciled to ancient law,
to the fathers so renowned for slow
progress to cymbal and to lute,

you might, if wishing were one voice
in tune with vision of the wise,
presume to nourish world, and raise
these love-slaves to their proper place.

*

310

If I could imitate those gentle white birds
drifting across the lake's face without trouble –
but there on earth's dark brow I still detect
enmired in mad concern my insane double.

————

Look, I am left to trance, my book closes,
the grave's machinations, the brain's invective
poison my air, but a banked grey cloud
repulses the gaze of the unholy detective.

*

311

The time strikes terror in my coward's heart.
I long for safety but my brain strangles
love's gentle offer, modest tongue's report.

The thin skin on old wounds rudely tingles
and leaping from one feared touch to the next
I yearn for the carnal danger of jungles.

It happens that when my eye has relaxed
and the crooked noise from the TV fades,
the date promised with the spirit is fixed.

On the roof the starlight blinds the cats.
Their egocentric vision turns on spikes
and flashes comedy through the reeds.

But the sequence of dreams of self evokes
traps and is trapped in concentric lines,
spinning what thread love's spider lacks.

The pattern tracked by disparate moons
into surface defined as passion's field
leaves the dance floor free for sober pains.

I am not the one my youth's ear called
the perfected one, truth's callous flirt
for whom nothing but you and elements ruled.

*

312

I am not happy with my sainted crown;
Too many passionate men can pull it down.

I fear the beast that rides my groin at night
and swallows stars, unmindful of my plight.

*

The curse is lifted and my dull eye shines.
Too much ethereal background was my shame.
Beneath an august sun my flesh reclines
and harvests love, though under some new name.

*

313

So much is done to please
the wind, the set of sail, the mind's
fairy tale emphasis on true love's blind

regret which has not surfaced yet,

that all our efforts trained towards love

must falter in wave and clot and flame
before the next moon draws its breath
or care consumes the flesh out there.

*

314

Soon Memory Weeps

The fountain leaps to flash the light
right down into the grotto's throat.
The candle flame is whipped by wind
that once ripped sail from Sinbad's boat.

The child is seated where the sun
is apt to burn or hold in thrall
and kittens must like tigers run
to catch their prey or lose it all.

Beyond the fringe of sky-clad hills,
ensconced within a battered shell,
the eunuch foetus fondly fills
his brain with news from book and bell,

while scent of wild carnation streams
down alleyways past horse and cart
to settle where Troy's Helen seems
impaled by the enchanter's art.

Oh balding poet, claim sweet fame
or cushion well thy fall from grace.
Soon memory weeps on stone for shame
or lies in state behind white lace.

*

315

During night's fascination has slipped
the yellowing moon and minstrels weep
to see such fondness for wandering gripped
in claws of death, in vice of sleep
but the time's champion stands equipped
with a scythe in the wheat field knee deep
in marigold and poppies, stripped
of honour whence his soul might leap

to join the choir of voices raised
in praise of promised joy and hope,
nor have his eyes but one time gazed
where gods as men alone may cope
unhindered, undriven by the crazed
momentum of the worldly trope –
and still his heart remains amazed
when Christ descends the temporal slope.

Meekly the foolish maids take drink,
lift skirts to show where man's source lies,
help plants to reason, beasts to think
that stars bleed morphine, stones grow eyes
to entertain, through symbol's chink,
the simple soul and the worldly wise,
since today love is driven to the brink
where heaven must fall and hell's weight rise.

*

316

Advent of winter weighs down mind,
    sickness concentrates the brain;
old age and decrepitude make
    confidence wane, strength break.

The joints swell, the tendons creak,
    magic threatens where I stand;
memory would stop to count the cost
    as if the Christ had fought and lost.

Muscles cramp, eyes dim,
    a beastly force urges death;
back and forth life's shuttle flits,
    intellect itself against life pits.

Always weakness sleeps in flesh,
    nowhere does the cockerel crow;
creeping cowardice leaves tracks,
    praises what man's nature lacks.

No one cares for fearful toil,
    labour among the born unkind;
only rebirth leaves fine traces,
    interpreted in exceptional cases.

*

317

Process

Oh how the wind and rain make these
limbs of mine throb with disease.
That is how I picture it for the time.
It seems I must exert my energies
in the direction of elements whose mass
refuses to let my king's train pass.

I fear the crowd who judge each metaphor
as though its presence meant some other thing.
Lovely illusion lets silver sleigh bells ring
to stir the heart, to make it shake snow off,
let ice crack, since that's where the law is hid.
Not sell each melted flake for the highest bid.

I am afraid to move a muscle; it may tighten
and leave me crippled, locked in some hard pain.
I want to race the children to the lamppost,
do cartwheels, wheelbarrows with them on the grass
and gradually celebrate the strength they gain,
not watch mine fade, perversely strained.

God has become flesh: that's where I take issue.
Perhaps I haven't understood that quite.
Surely that part of me that is racked should
take vantage somehow of god as blood.
I put it down to ignorance of myself
and secretly to an urge in my vocation.

Lie low: is god's counsel. Let my flesh think.
The moment you brood on mood or nightmare,
(hoping thereby to lay the issue bare)
the word singular and the world renowned
freeze one another out of countenance
and pain replaces these two hemispheres.

Vultures have pecked, eagles have ripped
all along, to clear the rot, and will do.
(A reason why we include all of mankind.)
The healing word and the tempting world
make one flesh, trustworthy to the point
where mystery clears the brain of confusion.

*

318

Cowardice tastes extremely bitter.

The loose change squandered on my soul
was dearly earned one day by fools.

I would stand opposed by no man's fancy,
willing to produce the natural requirement,
perfectly at ease among gods and beasts.

Oh cloud in man's eye, ever anew
risking the perfection slain at sunrise,
we too manage to harvest in sickness,
aloof in our ego under love's spell.

Born man, not fit for any lesser thing,
nor yet trustworthy beyond tried bounds,
tried by pain and diverse forms of death,
this seed of madness you preserve in your brain
will not die until your thoughts excuse you.

The involved wisdom rooted in the lamb's sphere
angers the wolf in his straight-line simplicity
and nowhere else is the sunlight apparent,
so repeat this craving for the saviour citizen
by all means, as often as your gorge rises –
your helpless efforts will never manage it alone.

*

319

The hyacinth blooms where the nettle stands
    attractive to the wide-eyed child.
    With bare arms it embraces both.

What monstrous urgency of life
has plucked, as though the gods were blind,
    response from the maternal gaze?

A breeze solicitous of love,
removes the danger from the child
and overrides the brain of science.

*

320

The Addict

Of course I am interested in my condition.

I want to clean myself up too
and step out on the town.

But I am too frightened to collect my wits
and if anyone were to ask me right now
who I am, I'd have to lie.

But I think I have some notion now
about the sort of work I do
and I'll try not to complain next time
when I'm assigned a painful task.

Pain can be hell, and that keeps me
on my toes, even though I
cannot come up with an intelligent idea,
an insight into how far I can do
and when should I let myself be done to.

As the drugs run out, panic sets in
because I have put my faith in chemicals,
though not entirely, I still have an ear out
for the message from those secret information centres
installed here and there by someone who loves me
and hopes I'll take the time out to tune in.

*

321

Your work is not achievement but believing
your promise holds. If anything is real,
your life both past and present, in achieving
your father's will, presents our commonweal.

In it you cope for us with all your suffering
even while we fear, endangered by our state.
In us you seek but this one self, one offering
in love held out, as we in knowledge wait.

Pain means you arrive, expecting us to make
some room here, not by death but by some deed,
example proved, no thing to make earth quake
or astonish men, but born forth from one seed

so small that no unhallowed eye might find it
or wrapped in awe, no soiled hand shall unwind it.

*

322

Would you say that the dance goes on
in spite of the grief we hide
or does the grief produce the dance
while we weep inside?

Does the action on the dance floor do
the dream down, compelling
flight from light into the light
and leave the tears upwelling?

Those are the interweaving realities
and we have the vision
required to move them or be moved
by them into fine condition.

But then the suffering of the pain
moves flesh to a tune,
builds body up before the eye
to picture the god triune.

Or so much sin and guilt
melts before flowers like snow,
or much more cumbersome it sits
insisting on saying no.

*

323

Can you hold out to the stars' might
while the eagle pauses in flight
and the flower, worse than dead,
blooms in your disappointed head?

Your nerves crave achievement,
your health an anodyne absurd
and the cruel mask would obscure
your face before my word is heard.

Account for the many false moves
made while under love's duress;
begin the conquest of inner space
and all fear of an early end repress.

You have stopped the dog's vicious mouth,
charmed the violent snake's blear eye;
now bask in the hale sun of god's love
while the clock makes its own time go by.

I am no moon, no morning cloud
veiling a light too pure to see.
None of my children speak out of turn
except they remove their hearts from me.

Trinkets will not pay, nor smiles do
where starvation requires the classic art,
or stretched, except for sinew and bone,
the aberrant flesh would fall apart.

*

324

It cannot be that our love grows old
bearing our happiness with it into death.
We dream beyond such mortal agonies
and spend ourselves, with each drawn breath,

for one whose legacy of love
is borne within us since we died
to right of law and strength of law
but also to the flesh untried.

So we really ought to search our hearts
for the timid judgment, the weak stance
in the face of our soul's comfort removed,
of stupid falsehood's bold advance.

The Christ within leaves not untouched
a single fibre of our being.
Organic love, resourceful love,
both question what our eyes keep seeing,

within us when hatred propagates our limbs'
seemingly irresponsible commotion
and the fear that hate will hurt us again
and spoil our brain's most favourite notion

of a blessed state on earth complete
with no hope needed for future dates,
no pleasure hunted by past days' guilt,
all death stopped by the life that sates.

But I think such a notion requires attention,
it beguiles us with a wrong feeling of our worth
and tends to drain our strength for withstanding
the most common tremblings of this earth.

We feel ourselves rewarded amply
for virtues practiced on the go
from hand to mouth, and such excitement
as we perceive would teach us so.

*

325

I have decided to change my life.
But this is no easy matter
since my will rides in a groove,
ignorant of other people's litter,
intent on an individual grave.

To start with I accept the truth
that love must risk its cushions.
If I incur the devil's wrath
by butting the world's fashions
I return, a wiser man, to my lathe.

But to translate theory into action
I must assume my spirit's vanity
and its desire to adhere to fiction.
Then eventually, in the vicinity,
my hand creates its own concoction.

And this too must be rejected
or somehow refitted into the plan
over the past two millennia attracted
by the spirit that makes all things groan.
The heart needs its wound inflicted.

Then finally this world feels real
and behind it god laughs proudly
because he loves an intemperate fool
who leaves himself open widely
to the force of the contemporary gale.

*

326

The deepest peace yet quakes
where branch rubs against branch
and an old rook croaks.

The sun splits the chaffinch.
The heat in the bark cracks,
dry leaves underfoot crunch

and then the new flame licks
the twigs black and eats.
The wayward child looks

at the moss between the roots,
recalls its first flight.
The hand at once locates

a stone of little weight,
(the eye aims) the bent arm
flings it at the stoat.

Acts such as this confirm
the reasoned root of love:
substance as pure form.

In the forest the children live,
each doing as it likes,
waiting for love to arrive.

*

327

I am not the man I was once
and how I grew, not always with an aim
might be worth recording some day,
if time allows, or time necessitates,
and whether the one or the other makes no difference
because we can fathom the depth of our concern
but never you mine, or I yours.

The purse I fill I can still give
and the mountains moved for me by well-meaning souls
weigh me down otherwise, elsewhere,
forced into that position as though
night did not follow day, day night,
its immensity as a problem overemphasized
since a single bird's eye suits it.

*

328

Lifting one leg across the style
he hesitates –
a wan smile
lifts its leg from the other side.

The effort of such a stance
eventually told.
A finch on a post nearby
winked its eye.

*

329

Oh let me not be timid in my heart,
to fear the bold move, the false start.
I would rather err and be corrected
than by my own brain vivisected.

*

330

Why has my hope gone
and the food it held out
to tiny mouths?

Why these uncouth
lip service testaments
to inert causes?

The ball floats,
not to descend but
anxiously awaited.

Where the hills meet
the sky's lucid blue,
our minds meet too.

*

331

I am so absorbed by my craft
or forced past perfect sight and sound
by an elementary drift
too fulsome to behold
as mirage courting morning star
within the sphere of crystal flowers

that the perfection of my might
leads downward to the moon's destruction.
So I would blend
Christ's blood with mine
and share in creature's dogged attempt
to flourish with an earthbound style.

*

332

A cold October day would fain
assume the burden of my voice,
disconsolate beyond description.

The sheer weight of my human nature
descends where rain collects in puddles,
drips gleaming off the plastic roof.

The clouds refuse to shape the sky
and so, half willing me to sleep,
my temper builds its sullen cage.

Passion is dragged in by the scruff
snarling, whipping me with its tail,
watched by an indecisive crew.

The asphalt street, the clay fields
give the impression they might lie
another season to support my eye.

*

333

A Glance behind the Scene

Why not, while of a more
cheerful disposition, touch upon
the cool mechanics of creation,
to maintain the interest of those
who appreciate a glance behind the scene.

If the hour strikes clarity,
that must be where the influence lies,
the force derives, where the word,
visually conceived in this case,
works and holds sway, reigns
or submits to some of its manifestations.

Only a crude, unfeeling person would
remain insensitive to such an appeal,
surely the desire of fresh life itself
to make itself still more free
by leaping to some identity,
perhaps across.

Required of me or you? Hardly more than
loving attention, supply of limb,
above all belief that this is so:
the conceptual bone assumes imagined flesh,
and there's our example!

*

334

So much daylight lies out there
on wet roofs and on glistening tiles
so splendid, so surpassing fair,
    and buildings oh, these monstrous piles

    of stone that lasts and will not fail,
for man has laid it each on each
in modest spirit, not for sale
    to greed or power beyond his reach;

    and such machines as would astound
dear god himself if he but knew,
for speed below, above the ground
    or chasing all the demons through

    and works of art so mighty that
our flesh becomes spiritual grace
on contact – angels marvel at
    our cleverness from outer space.

So when I look at all these things
I hardly can believe my eyes,
what happiness appearance brings –
    but then I say: the daylight lies.

*

335

The city breaks all rules and laws
but knows not that the law holds true.
Beyond its contest with itself
it knows no other thing to do

except to kill, with blind eyes shut,
the dove, the tiger and the snake
and then to rue these public deeds.
The city, like a soft snowflake,

descends and lands on cultural stone
and comes to rest in crystal shape
if seen up close, and then dissolves.
Some idols manage still to drape

their cloaks of magic over man's
more infinite proportionate drives,
to give this spirit time to heal
before the city's prince arrives

and allocates, endowed with might,
the gifts civilian man has craved.
If anyone still doubts this truth
the city may have *him* enslaved.

*

336

The Wedge

So far we have nothing to complain about,
only character assassination on the street
and once in a while,
left to ourselves,
we create moments of cracked silence.

Therefore we should gradually lead up to
the plague on Main Street before nine
and a suitable occasion
presents itself
as soon as we immunize against pain.

*

337

My Gentle Friend

The meek shall inherit the earth.
I crave meekness like water
and know what my life is worth.
Meanwhile my spirits cater
to illusions backed by strife.
If I crack the world's pewter
will that get me a fresh loaf?

If I rush about screaming abuse,
afraid not to raise the roof
with gestures that look too nice,
and at night the moon bites
chunks out of the human race
because my loving never rates,
how can any man survive?

A man is what he eats,
so I eat what Christ is and rove
on pastures benignly green
in love with beauty, or in love
with this gentle friend of mine
who joins me beside the hearth
and renews my love again.

*

338

Love's Easy Tricks

Much subtlety's required to show the simple heart
in its pure grasp of delight fetched
on the wing here, there in continuing
grace upheld, cradle to rock baby in.

The technique that goes, softly and gently, into the
nursing of the will as gift offered,
a thing happy though narrow in its abiding
reference instilled, lacks all mutation.

Instead, there, live in love's luxury lap,
rosehips giggling under an early snowfall,
bluetit bouncing from twig to willow twig –
a roomy performance, kindly look at it.

And share, more than share, make known to
sundry and all how the sun's pleasure sits
easy, willingly, near you, here you may
build it, on it build, nearly self willed.

But cruel hands have an organized crime-rated
achievement, the eye sated prior to its
tending of heart's fire, so guard, ward off on
hilly domain silly life's spurious gain.

*

339

Poison

I am not moody, for no man's lust brings
vision to bear on my more vital parts.
This vision so transcends the luck I experience
and stays there in the upper stratosphere

that the coach-loads of words eventually ripe
before the sense, must aggravate the loser
of temperament at large – hence the design
praised by the critic, formerly the idealist.

*

340

Even the over-emphasis striving
in bush and bloom to waylay the eye,
(so that no tragedy may occur
nor the light operate in idleness)

drinks in, makes more suitable
the pictured cottage on the slope
or strikes a balance, knowingly
between the hard heart and the cruel brain.

*

341

The violet hides between roots,
the sky presses down.

———

The swifts scream overhead
round the antique cathedral.

*

342

Rain patters on the Perspex roof.
The clock ticks within the skull.
Under my bum the chair creaks.
A silence into my mind leaks.

*

343

Why we project ourselves
far into the night
puzzles me. Why not hold
tight to a few
facts that would let us

bridge the abyss
instead of roaming
straight into the dark?
The illumined soul draws
strength from any old spark.

*

344

Could you train your hand to sing,
your mind to ring from stone soft sounds,
the flighty angels to shame?

I could hollow out the stone
alone with the voice trained methodically
and flighty angels would aid me.

*

345

Only in this language speaks the proportionate
rhythm we feel when our blood
dreams its own, its own end in pretending
to what the law's ghost must fulfil.

Once by assignment of stars, language set
muted tradition up there, drew
breath in reflection, pointed to man, stinted
on no human nature, good or ill.

*

346

If language were down where
shock treated shock and
the high wind took stock of
life's routine acquisition

these perfect proofs of night
trapped between glass and glass
would turn fully round and
plead with man for admission.

*

347

What? Look behind.
Make a song dance, a dance
spring from the wind; let blind

parlance flow ignominiously
to stop ears demanding
a franchise on sense.

*

348

Passion Regained

Where do the hills begin, the valleys,
    to simplify their appeal, where do
moth-eaten eagles study the breeze, work
    wings with pulleys to earn some ease,

except where the year, the age ends, or
    trouble ends too, where suitably still
faces fill the journals, empty the brains.
    Our trust bears us aloft anew.

Trust has exceptional value as, more
    than security's home as finder's keepers
will-o'-the-wisp eternal look to the
    future that ends, has snow on boughs

through centuries tested, and yet, fling
    arms out, pennies on cobbled street,
there stands, hands in pockets, the grand
    revolution explored, the ignored spirit.

We have energy more than enough, only
    cowards spring for the thing in our
prisons with talent saturated, they
    cling like moss, nevertheless dancing

across meadows in the nude, looping
    their moral majority where the eye fits,
because the problem holds their attention
    and more we dare not now mention.

*

349

TV

The problem our time refuses to face,
beckoning death, deadly invention,
the mild purgative of truthful sound
might cure; a pleasantry, a good intention,

but our frosty delight in mad refrains
performed to ruin action's path
shall know no cure, but only this:
dimmed eyesight's conscious aftermath.

*

350

Out of the dark creeps
the dull spirit of the earth
to be illumined here among men
for an age, a time, a turn.

Forgotten by men it rises
beyond the scope of men, beyond
to outstrip their perspicacity,
their longing for everlasting winter.

When one thing seems to be another,
or usurps its place, given up unwillingly,
danger must figure in human plans
and a dark sky requires reference.

So beat, beat down, down into
turf and clay the moody resistance offered,
the thrice-linked reply to all
action shored against the living tree.

I am no masked intruder
appearing near the exposed rock
to warn of the eagle's claws, the bears
crushing ferocity, or a child's terror.

But my arm points, even contrary
to the feelings my heart might harbour,
even parallel to panic rooted behind
the fourth rib, to the plague of a thirst.

Genius feeds time-honoured
expectations, but an art trades
gold for the wind's power, activity
for sick imprisonment in disease.

If we were to exhaust all our arts,
still would remain the luck of the
right arm, prosperity's perpetual influence,
or some tame animal would rescue us.

But believe how the sun's circle sits
crown-like upon man's hallowed head;
how man's organs give again
an orderly substance, to shape or build.

*

The Pursuit of Knowledge

The pursuit of knowledge has this in common
with the centuries' march towards future goals:
a silence at the heart, imperturbable,
and the unflinching, steady gaze of the man.
Here we exercise the faculties of our spirit,
there we infringe upon rites of worship,
caught up in the search for the appropriate value,
trembling before him whose might we suspect
and certain of one thing only: our relation.

The discovered skill, during needful employment,
called art, held in readiness, to train the sense,
would sometimes practice manhood of its own accord,
steeped in tradition, not by care of consequence
overly inhibited, and then the trading begins,
tender emotions fly to the wall, charisma speaks
of another nobility, the night illuminates itself
in deepest responsibility, not outworn fashion –
so reject the suggestion of an ape ancestry.

Where the world collapses into itself, men lose
the knack for self-preservation and they worry about
money and love, and the mind's stillness.
What animals take for granted, the shape of plants,
the wealth of minerals in their crystal linkage,
men despise because it stems from another source,
not from the pride's lust stopped or started,
not from a thoughtless moment's urgency
and the will to reflect kills the will to ponder.

Love, the principle of life and the living,
contacts the brittle youth and tests him,
shows him the type, by example and sign,
of aim and missile, cast and goal,
lifts him out of himself for a moment's pleasure
of the sort no memory likes to unwind
and presents the unsuspecting heart with a choice:
follow here now, in these absolute footsteps
or repeat some reflection in some animal eye.

Given the heart moves towards its maker,
rejects the shame of the unpopular motive,
much is promised, as though it stood in glory.
The future looms everywhere unannounced,
transforms the breath of the delinquent soul,
appeals to weaknesses, stresses faults.
The flight starts, from death, over landscapes
troubled by sleep, dreamt by a worldly lot
whose fingerprints soil the abstaining glass.

Man is first loved, then loves. His existence
precedes any effort he makes to know himself;
and then, this knowledge, oh, if it lasts
too long, how can it help but prevent him?
Son of poor man, reluctant to be raised up,
discards his glory, hopefully for a good cause
and arrives nevertheless, though probably unawares.
Some learn love, in whose agony love bears
witness to the man, whose world all encounter.

Instinct for truth, rooted in the riverbed,
difficult to expunge, though many succeed,
and this success, born of a hollow love,
wears and tears away the peace of a nation.
Guilt must pursue him who is blind to it,
materialist progress must lure the uprooted
naturally to his destruction, lest he interfere
with the law of laws, in love perfected.
No one returns who has disowned his heart.

Heart to those in the West means one thing:
conscience, courage; an understanding love.
Trials in the East stem from the heart too
though here the society of men absorbs them.
Individual logic troubles our image,
but all men touch either good or evil,
with a will or by chance, and all have freedom.
The technique worth interest is how we love
each time we assent to life's precious burden.

Dogs run in packs through our culture's alleyways
and the dead startle by the force of their expression.
Routine symbols mark the opened graves
where the smell of fresh upturned earth lingers.
Dancers surround the lower-strewn craters
chipped from the crust, for imponderable reasons.
Meanwhile one's mind may absorb the light of day,
eternity from the most unexpected quarters:
a vision facing vision – love merging with a love.

* * *

352

The way we all praise, confess or complain,
not only poets, artists and professional men
but housewives, caretakers, I and you,
makes sense, if it's done honestly and true.

No need to pretend to be someone else
much better to pretend you are who you are,
then gradually you too come to believe it:
you can be yourself as soon as you achieve it.

*

353

Naïve

Most people want culture to
confirm them in their suspicions that
reality is a trumped up thing and
to harden them in their resolve,
to back them up in their belief,
that the truth is a lot of foolishness.

Therefore I call it vicious when
anyone, for whatever reason, be it
popularity or financial gain,
tries to tell people what will please them
where they hold fast to such a belief
and while they labour under such a resolve.

*

354

Must let love transform,
with him at my right elbow,
whatever comes my way;
trust, for example, that it all fits,
before the act.
For once we forget about conquest
of new territory, and sit back
hands open.

Difficult to believe how
easy the work proceeds,
love simply gulping time down,
me directing the mouth to the food,
keeping the heart turning over,
the head cool.
Practice makes perfect here too
so never quarrel with details
but concentrate on the performance,
look to your various notions of success.
While the drive for perfection exists,
no one need lose hope,
nor should any man justify
a future furnished with less than
the goods he bargained for
at a time when his blood still
warmed to comets, to fallow deer
grazing before dawn near woods
and a shot rang out
destroying the mind's noise

so that we all learn what it means
to sit tight and expect the independent
hand on the shoulder, the curse
rocking the ear and the wallowing
passion, there, as an elephant tricked out,
remnants of dream in the gut.

We probed the entire organisation of life,
erected huts in among the fruit trees,
looked up saints' names in volumes of
parchment three feet thick, as though
that might change the wind's direction.

What became of the audiences, one asks.
Carefully staked out as the real estate appeared,
we hopped on no bandwagon, po-
litically speaking, but went on with
each day distinct from the next, did our
shopping, made coffee, looked at snapshots
and happily watched the babies grow
up into strapping youngsters,
full of piss and vinegar and
a taste for Jesus, so it please you.

Goodness crept in on hands and knees,
snuck in on tip-toe, so it did,
dressed up to raise hell,
cheered by passers-by who
refused to countenance the contradiction:

of hooliganism in the sanctum spiritual,
of high jinks over and above individual
allotment.

There stood the tiger's servants,
surrounding the tiger himself,
lips curled back, teeth moist.

One mentions these things because
rather than crow about conquest
the human mind would share its tranquillity.

I achieve what the sun achieves, consciously.

* * *

355

I may not suggest the sea unless
that part of our organization behaves
abstractly which gives the fullest possible
occasion for image-making and an intense
feeling for the justice of separate minds.

But the cool rock clings to our
much more degenerate souls and casts
aspersion where cloud shifts all manner of
taste and attention, even beyond the point
of local permanence and isolated humour.

*

356

Count the ways
folded into the stick's bark
and hearken unto the
created mood, for love's sake,

though beneath much
prohibited custom and strife
an illusion of a love hides
less magical than pure.

Or can anyone create,
if the mood strikes him, these
careful considerations
prepared under influence?

*

357

So far it appears before
eyes not tranquil nor
captured within spheres

that an image shall reign
roundly where the earth's
people look to their life.

While an exact replica of
the human mind cannot
achieve the flower's own

terror at random justice,
still we opt out of beauty
and lead our pride on.

*

358

My image teaches: be of good cheer,
let lines on face point way to mirth,
your face assemble as god's face,
even as though by some outward grace
the air could raise and resurrect.

Happiness makes us circumspect.

*

Good luck, my friend ...

Of all the illusions that spring from a debased mind
perhaps this one ought to draw our attention most
readily, least reluctantly, straight into the mouth
by illusion itself defined, and perhaps, too,
while the trembling spheres exert their influence,

we would do well beneath this leafy bower, kept
warm and safe by thoroughgoing thought, stript
of all pretension, mask and false timidity,
to locate within the organic needle's eye our own
test of strength, unique set purpose, wise intention.

Good fellow man, we limit our pleasant laughter
to animal concern, our irony flaps in the wind as though
an intrinsic particularity, invisible by force of
definition to the naked eye, spoke for our weak hearts,
left our forts and ports to the enemy, to his mercy.

What we remain mindful of on a Sunday may speak
up for us some other day, or this way in reverse.
What we calmly accept, though terrified expressly
beneath the calmer gaze of witless, guiltless eyes,
builds up meanwhile an edifice of trust for us.

So good luck, my friend, may you lie beautifully
receptive at the bottom of some well, eyes fastened
to the round hole expressive of some starry sphere.
I look for your tombstone, hew it from memory's
imponderable quarry, set it upon your insensate flesh.

*

360

Do temples still weigh down the earth
and men's minds captivate
what springs from hate, leaps from
unmindful stone, and do we dare,
drive bargains, so as not to lapse
perhaps into civilized confusion?

I know, but make no attempt to
calculate the flood's increment.
I perceive, but vainly do not stir,
hoping some thing may occur to lift
the burden to another man's back.
I struggle, therefore, against myself.

The widest scope includes the beam
rotating from the lighthouse. This
ministerial 'point of view', this fourth
person invented to give an alleged
deity the care, the worry and tears,
spirits our fears away uselessly.

We are given two hands with which
to do, not weave magic spells, trading
illustrious gesture for false hope.
The queer notions our brains pick up
instil night's awful tempests here,
textual proof of a dangerous mission.

*

One waits for you where the poplars stream
in single file along the road's edge,
or there, among water's dark turbulence,
finished within the dull eyes' sphere,
by the broken reed as yet unannounced,

time's radiant saviour would work wonders,
in advanced Science build golden images
or, fenced off behind tradition's wire,
perplexed as though to capture some affection,
this Modern Hero playacts for the masses.

Nothing may move or be moved where he gazes.
Some characteristic weaknesses recommend him
to bound charity, some flavour of being
despised, forsaken by friends, brings
his case to within a handshake's proximity

and strangely he does find some sympathy
among blood relations, dependent upon him
lately for some certificates of licence:
general permits to express the womb's malice
as though therein lay some comforting sanction.

The search for truth out there, uninhibited
by a false passion, by distorting mistrust,
suspicion nursed within the cowardly heart,
reveals at times some less familiar fashion
of abstract thought, of concrete suffering,

so that reality's all-embracing shelter
is left behind, for some vicarious king's
damaging touch, promising recognition
to weed among weeds, but inclining, in fact,
to promiscuous feeling and damning act.

*

362

While tribal strife still haunts this separate isle
I'll bide my time and stick to truth a while.

But no, some say, go out before time fails
and meet the world whose fame our heart entails.

Pretend out there some fortune sits and waits,
prone to neglect the man who hesitates.

*

363

Trace to its origin
this curious pain,
this bewildering weakness
for an unhinged brain.

Strip of all honour
the counsel it gives
and delay no further
while the true mind lives.

Seek out the energy
supplied in fits and starts
to the body politic
by diverse arts,

then inject with charm
all ill-gotten gains
and reject for a failure
whatever else remains.

*

364

Help me, oh queen of silence and of wonder,
I am torn towards the deep, my spirit
moves as upon land cracked by heat
and the power I once enjoyed is lost to me.

Nowhere do I see the refreshing vision,
past all expectation my instincts reflect
the horrors of a strange life, the obscurities
enlisted by a promiscuous eye.

Never again will I entrust my emotions to
a public gaze unwilling to discriminate
between the roar of the sea and the sand's
still passage through the inverted hourglass.

Now some rest leads me to my conclusion;
as a roof over my head it proves
sanctuary from the cruel, no, provoked
light of lights, limited in outlook.

If our nerves were allowed to rule us only
all would be lost, so therefore we enervate
the sinewy character bent on our destruction
with a show of excitement, and a sword's blade.

*

365

The habit of long hours spent

servile at the feet of reality
is hard to break. We can't
quite trust anyone's ability
except our own to see us through
because we lack the credulity,
the ruthless patience to fight free

of memories planted in our past,
now choking the experience of the day;
of our plans' numbing frost
or the lazy drift into the dark,
devoid of all human interest.
We bob up and down like a cork
on financial securities. We reckon

we can curb our habits, but they irk
others more than us; they sicken
our wives and children to the point
where they cry out. We have forsaken
our senses because they acquaint
us with some special affront
to the pride we nourish in our mind.

*

366

Someone rallies the nations' support.

Flights of lap-winged birds were observed
calmly transcending the world's oceans.

Space beckons to tie men's abiding
intellect and haply to reverse their will
since world gives shape here to the body.

Tribes cross borders at night to flee from
one type of oppression, transplanting terror
until no mind dares signify by gesture
of voice or deed the perennial union.

For example the mind's hollow tribute
paid for no reason to an empty sky,
with a resonance all its own, jangles
until the heart grows too sick of so much
vile festivity to deny it an identity.

The earth's arch enemy too would have us
build scaffolding to climb brown towers
erected to last a timeless century
while the trumpets blared, needless spears
pierced needful flesh, fairly invited
by endless provocation, the curs of life.

*

Experience and Belief

Belief knows no bounds, it
lies in its nature to range freely
everywhere, we who do it
not excluded. Experiment gives it
intensity. We draw, for example,
away from the senses, to show how
perfectly happy, eventually,
sense can make us, or the passions need
some disguised entertainment, since
here, as elsewhere, work makes a profit,
stimulates life, removes barriers
set up to provoke the removal.

It helps to believe intimately
what our organs present, since we
have what it takes to discriminate
automatically, this lovely ideal force,
and those who have not, need us to lead,
urge and shelter them.
Of course by the time
they believe it, we have suffered our way
through to a timelier wisdom again.

And belief
makes no judgment
but lets itself be judged
offering no contradiction.

We do, after all, have
creation out of nothing,
though it seems
matter from emotion makes change,
or the image, spawned in association,
would lead to a thing or two,
meaning a kind of magic – which
craft men reject since it rises
from unclean origin, conceived
hatefully and in haste,
though the young apprentice
tests his mettle here, distinguishing
image from picture, superstition from
understanding pure and simple.

Belief leaves magic to one side,
strides on ahead through confusion, confident
though the air goes rare, that nowhere danger
means death rather than sharpened wits,
tempered trust. It casts no aspersion,
never titillates for taste's sake, nor brings
partial forms of life into disrepute.

Now experience has its hands full these days,
let me tell you, because nothing's impossible
and nearly everything inexpedient.
The popular thrust of opinion through public space
lets many a love relationship languish,
crowds out the sinister to further cheap interest,
praises to destroy, converts gold into silver,
silver into brass, in short
devalues by dint of approval.

Experience is stretching out feelers on purpose,
antennae with intent; not lip-service to
love in the laboratory, but edge of the
ego with the grain into the split, the
sealed self soaring inviolate where
god only knows to strip off insolence.

It means like this: This is my body,
or otherwise: this is my blood. No diatribe
can inherit that doctrine and spoil it.
No wishful thinking, up- or below-stairs,
can turn it into madness, madcap tactics,
active service. We have achieved, gentlemen,
the illusion of the times; we have
crept through the ditch, cut the barbed wire,
planted the charges – years ago, really,
which is why so many forgot. Small wonder.

This then means: experience in action,
'the achieve of, the mastery of the thing' or
down in the heart, settled as gold dust,
ready for spring cleaning –

which means progress too, in the only way
those know who like to live life timeless.
Congratulate the heavy-hearted few,
they experience for our sake.

*

368

Under the extraordinary influence of nocturnal muse
the sky danced with fire,
and slowly rotating around its axis, the mind's
minister, with perfection illuminate,
presented the flesh with the requisite spectacle.

Some fashionable men excused this as an aberration
brought on by too much wine,
and the elderly lady who lives near the sandstone
chapel and chain-smokes maintained
she could cure, if given halve a chance, the financial
incubus, with the touch of a sensitive
finger, as though testing the proven loaf.

The point to be made in public simply
centred on the need for the given act, not in
deference to some sign, or drawing upon
such sweetness as might merely repeat the illusion
for assurance, but disabused of the
tasteless generality, homeward bound under its
own steam, saturated by the particular.

*

369

I cannot
explain my mind
    properly, I feel,
with no doubt left over.

I cannot
root out the evil that
    sits explaining its
self as though that
    counted.

If I quarrel with
    simple men,
hopeful of some ex-
    planation of what
they mean,

I soon come away
    thwarted,
fishhook hanging
    empty from
disappointed line.

*

370

Much I give out for others, of whatever persuasion,
carefully shrouded in obscure thought,
so as to step ever so lightly through the thicket,
the congenital blindness, brought on by
generations of uninformed discontentment;

some I leave here for a few who
require no substitute and know when the wind blows
so that all is said in confidence to them,
under no cloak of visible invisibility, but
here so clear that light suffices;

while the rest I keep under wraps, of no use
to anyone but myself, waiting the time out,
lacking no earthly goods whatsoever, reliant upon
selfsame strength as ever distinguished,
heartfelt humanity upon a cloud of unknowing.

*

371

That I am but illogical and plain,
  not suited to the finer lusts,
    gives me but little pain,
since wood rots and iron rusts.

While the trivial tale goes unmended
  across footbridge self-refined,
    the world's history tended
      to corrupt my mind.

* * * * *
* * *
*

Index of first lines

188

* * * * *

* * *

*